LIFELINE:

Defeating Depression and Suicide Among Teens & Young Adults

LIFELINE:
DEFEATING DEPRESSION AND SUICIDE AMONG TEENS & YOUNG ADULTS

Project : Your Life Matters

KRYSTA L. COVINGTON

XULON PRESS

Xulon Press
2301 Lucien Way #415
Maitland, FL 32751
407.339.4217
www.xulonpress.com

© 2021 by Krysta L. Covington

All rights reserved solely by the author. The author guarantees all contents are original and do not infringe upon the legal rights of any other person or work. No part of this book may be reproduced in any form without the permission of the author.

Due to the changing nature of the Internet, if there are any web addresses, links, or URLs included in this manuscript, these may have been altered and may no longer be accessible. The views and opinions shared in this book belong solely to the author and do not necessarily reflect those of the publisher. The publisher therefore disclaims responsibility for the views or opinions expressed within the work.

Unless otherwise indicated, Scripture quotations taken from the King James Version (KJV) – public domain.

Printed in the United States of America

Paperback ISBN-13: 978-1-66281-570-6
Ebook ISBN-13: 978-1-66281-571-3

DEDICATION

I dedicate this book to everyone who has helped make the events possible, who have given me encouragement to keep going even after so many negative attacks from other people. Thank you so much for believing in me and having a heart for this cause concerning suicide and depression among teens and young adults. Thank you so much for having a vision and a true dedication to a project such as this. Words can't express how grateful I am for all of my friends and family who have come out to events, who have donated money, time and energy, and shared posts.

I dedicate this book also to all the teens and young adults I have helped and will come to help through this program. I'm hopeful you continue to stay encouraged on your journey through life. I want you to know you mean so much to me and I'm so grateful I could be a part of a positive process of healing and restoration in your life. Please keep persevering and believing. Just know everyone who has made this possible has your back. We are here for you and we believe you can do amazing things in your life. Keep pushing, keep fighting!

Thank you so much, friends and family. May the Lord bless you richly for all your efforts and time and involvement in this project for mental health: Project Your Life Matters Defeating Depression and Suicide Among Teens and Young Adults.

A special thank you to all my friends and family and everyone who has made Project Your Life Matters possible. My prayer is that this book is an inspiration and blessing to all who read it.

Lynnese Covington; Damien McAllister; Michael Philips; Doug Douglas; Deontre Finklea; Michael Lowe; Aaron Jones; Jessica Mitchell; Lashell Harrison; Aaron Covington Michael Jones; Phillip Berry; Brenda White and Antoine White; Kenneth Longmire; Michael Major; Larry Worsley; Ronta Black; Dominic Griffin; Romika Johnson; Jonathan Davis; Mimi Lenay; Sheldon Hawkins; Darreous Moody; Nate Mitchell; Donald Smith; Charles McCarthy; Agner Quisol; Isacc Sparrow; Dyrome Everette; Llano Deloatch; Micheal Cavicante; Chris Anthony; James Hawk; Steven Jones; Shantel Thompson; Quran Floyd; Niko Crittenden; James; Boris Johnson; Chris White; Jordan Joy Rodgers; Chantika Brown; Morris Jacobs; Seanara Earl; Tazewell Pierce; Kerry Seawright; Steve John Covington; Carolyn Seawright; Carolyn Reid; Laramie Klein; Yvonne Seawright Brooks; Kevin D. Parker, ED.S; Camisha Walker; Lakia Harris; Shavonn Hayes; Christopher Sanchez; Quatasia Jones; Bobby Cross; Tyla Jones; Tasha Lee; Daniel Clark; Quisha Jones; Bernadette Fisher; Trevor Alladin; Chris White; My cousins, Sam, Jason, Alicia, Nikki, Aaron, Rhasheem; Jermaine Bellamy; Johnathan Perry; Jonathan Davis; Cydell McCord; Jermaine Savage; Edgar Smith; Jason Walker; Brendan Salas; Nikki Guappa; Shamar Reed; Vincent Daniels; Darius Southern; Jacoby Mathis; Christina M. Fisher; Alexander, aka Boss; DeAngelo Barnes; Sharnette Jordan; Rachel Smith; Tony Wilson; Carmi Nola; Net Barrow; DayJasha Jordan; Henderson Cunningham Jr.;

Dedication

DEE-BEATS; Carl Lowe; Timothy Wiggins; Lorenzo Martin; Summertime Madden; Amerika Williams; Pop Gambino; Brianna McKeown; Savion Hays; Elijah Pierce, Pauline Pierce, Zacchaeus Pierce; Cobi Hinton; Christopher Davis; Lakisha Campbell; Jessica Mitchell; Rick Sanchez; Charles Anthony; Folashade Amure-Oshin & Victor Oshin; Winston Tillett; Randy Hassell Jr;

A special thanks to all the businesses that donated and supported LifeLine Project Your Life Matters. I was very humbled to see so many businesses willing to jump in on helping me prevent suicide and depression in our community. I'm so thankful for your partnership and dedication to causes to improve mental health. You believed in my cause more than some of the people I would have expected to support me. So a special thank you to all of the staff, ministries, employees and customers who were involved in Project Your Life Matters, Defeating Depresson and Suicide among Teens and Young Adults.

IHOP - Lisa Counts
Buffalo Wild Wings - Ryan Barongan
Kate Christie: Meal Fundraising
Dave & Busters - Tina Rhondes
Office Depot- Aaron Mesham
No Sleep Entertainment:
Julian Norwood- Brandy Mark's
Christain Way Ministries -Pastor David & Britani Martinez
Newport News City Park - Lindsey Carrol
TeenLine - Cindi Berns
Andrea Chardis - Illustrator
Peninsula Family Skating Center

Cherished Ministries - Carlie Gabbert & Christina Montgomery

Thank you so much everyone. I appreciate everyone's efforts, everyone's encouragement. Thank you to my mother and my sisters, my grandmother, my uncle and my beautiful daughter. To all my nieces & nephews I love you so much!

I'm so appreciative to the Lord for laying this on my heart, because I believe one of our missions in this life is to reach back and touch lives in a positive way. I also dedicate this book to my brother, Rodney Covington, and my two brothers who passed away a few years back, Ryan and Raymond Seawright. To all of my nieces and nephews. And also to our grandfather who passed away in 2020, Chester Seawright. My aunt Alice and my uncles who passed away, Gary and Albert Covingotn, you are in my memories forever. I love you!

Thank you so much to everyone who has been a blessing to me.

TABLE OF CONTENTS

What is a Lifeline? 1
Pandemic 6
Your Life Matters 10
You are Amazing 12
Anxiety and Mental Battles 15
Opposition 21
A Father's Betrayal 26
But The Lord was with Me! 38
Pain and Suicidal Thoughts 43
We are More than our Pain 49
Depressions Terror 58
What are you Grateful for? 60
Necessary Obstacles 65
Rejection 70
Unbothered 80
The Bigger Picture 84
Your Life has Value 86
Small Accomplishments Still Count 88
Bumps in the Road 90

Make the World Your Runway 95
Life is a Battle you Can Win 97
Powerless or Powerful. 100
Having Hope in Hopelessness 103
Tragedies and Triumph. 113
Faith 115
Gratitude 120
Are You Just Existing? 122
Choose Life. 125
True Happiness 128
Warning Signs of Depression. 130
Prayers for Peace and Freedom 133
Signs When Your Child is Depressed 141
Help Resources for Teens and Young Adults 143
Conclusion 159
References. 163

WHAT IS A LIFELINE?

What is a lifeline exactly? And where can you find it? A lifeline is something to hold to save a drowning or falling victim. It's also an effort or organization you can aid, to lend a helping hand, rescue, and/or support a person. A lifeline can be physical, mental or spiritual. In my life experiences with battling depression, I needed all three. I was drowning in life, trying to make sense of my existence, feeling constantly overwhelmed by everything and everyone. I needed a lifeline in the form of a mental rescue. On the outside I seemed fine, but on the inside I was hiding so much pain, hurt, regret and fear.

I grew up in the 90s and early 2000s. My childhood was rough and my teen years were even worse. I was ridiculed all throughout elementary school, teased and made fun of most of middle school, and in high school I was just a joke. Trying to go to my parents about the issues was difficult, because to them they were petty issues that could easily be solved by either ignoring them or telling the teacher. I think it's universal for parents to respond in the same way.

"Kris, just ignore those kids in your class."

"Tell the teacher or the principal."

This is good advice, but what I really think I wanted to hear as a child, but I didn't know how to express it then, was: "Kris, you are not the things that people call you. You are beautiful and you are special in so many ways. I know these words are hurtful, but you shouldn't believe them.

At that time in my life, I believed every ugly word they called me had to have some truth to them. If they didn't, then why were they teasing me? My logic as a kid was it had to be true. That was why they were teasing me. Nothing else made sense. So like most kids, I told half the story to my parents, hoping they could read between the lines of my pain. I hoped they would give me something verbally to reassure me I was special, I wasn't this waste of space, and I had value.

I couldn't really express myself to the extent I needed to let my mother know I was hurting really badly, emotionally. At the same time, I honestly didn't want to make a huge deal out of it, for fear of possible embarrassment from my classmates knowing I told my mom about everything. So I pretended to either not be bothered by the constant harassment at school, or if I mentioned anything to her, I made it sound so not a big deal, so she wouldn't be upset.

I get the response my parents had toward the issues. I purposely made light of everything and they never really knew exactly how I felt or what was really going on, because I didn't want a scene at school. What's worse than being teased is being known for snitching to your parents or teachers. Kids can be so cruel, and they have very sneaky ways of hiding their abusive tactics so adults don't know what's happening. We all have probably experienced a situation where we were being kicked under the desk when the teachers turned their backs to the class.

So my self-esteem was nonexistent at this point. I carried this low self-esteem throughout my childhood, which only allowed more situations of pain to happen that I felt somehow I deserved. I was depressed most of my childhood, trying to let things roll off my back. Basically I just pushed all the hurts and pains to the back of my mind.

I tried so hard to pretend nothing bothered me, but deep down it was damaging my overall outlook on life and who I was as a person. I became this very shy, timid girl who couldn't talk without trembling. A girl who felt so scared to even look anyone in the eye directly. I believed I was ugly and worthless. So with all the negative words I heard most of my life circulating through my mind, I felt like I was too ugly to even speak to anyone and make eye contact. It's the saddest thing in the world to be so mentally and emotionally defeated you lose your sense of self-worth. I carried this burden of pain for years and it affected my entire life.

For anyone who has been emotionally scarred like this or similar ways in life, I'm here to tell you: Hold your head up high. You are not worthless, you are special, you are unique, and you are more than your physical appearance. You have talents and abilities and you have purpose in this world. I can tell you this confidently, because no one is a mistake. You were born on purpose with a purpose. The lies of cruel people don't define who you are. I want you to start healing today from anything in your life that has put you down or made you feel unimportant. I speak life, love, happiness and joy over your life right now. You are so important. Don't let haters steal your joy.

I want people from all walks of life who are affected by suicidal thoughts or depression to find hope, healing, and restoration in their lives. I want you to know you're not alone in the despair and all the pain and anxiety you may be suffering. I'm giving my experience and my research, my love, my heart, and my care for everyone who has suffered with mental health issues. I get you and I understand. I began this journey of healing through a program I started in my local community of Virginia Beach, Virginia.

Lifeline: Project Your Life Matters, Defeating Depression and Suicide Among Teens and Young Adults.

I felt the need to share my story and journey to help kids, teens and young adults out of suicide and depression. I know I'm only one person, but one person can make an impact in a positive way. If I can help one child, one teen, one adult out of depression and help prevent suicide and give someone a positive perspective in life, I will be so grateful! I believe my story will help many and I hope my words of inspiration and love motivate you to stand with me to help others out of depression and prevent suicide.

I dedicate this book to everyone who has lost a loved one to suicide, and I pray you join me in this mission of saving lives. The lives lost to suicide will never be forgotten and my sincere hope is to help young people heal and reach back out in their own communities and start a positive change for future generations.

I have partnered with LifeLine National Suicide Hotline and TeenLine Teens Helping Teens, getting the word out about support groups in areas all over the United States that provide help for anyone suffering with depression. This book is full of useful advice, information, resources, numbers to call or text, and references to different help centers, along with down-to-earth heart-to-heart stories. These are things I've experienced throughout my life and ways I have become a stronger person today, how I defeated depression, suicidal thoughts, and anxiety.

I include helpful natural ways to reduce stress, positive self-talk, and encouragement throughout the process. While you read this book, I suggest you grab a journal and write down different things that come to mind as you go through each chapter. This book is all about healing and restoration. I want to inspire new joy and happiness in your life, which doesn't just come through everything being perfectly right. I want to help you develop a new appreciation for yourself and everything that makes you who you are.

This is a journey of self-discovery to hope, love and oneness with your past, present and future. We are not victims of our circumstances, hurts, pain, or failures. I want you to envision yourself strong, because you really are. You are strong and you have everything you need right within you to tap into your full potential right where you are in life. I can't wait to read your emails and stories and hopes and dreams. My mission is to help you realize there is more to life than drama, pain, and disappointment. I want you to start living instead of existing. Life is too precious to sit on the sidelines defeated, hopeless, and full of self-doubt.

You can be happy even when you have a bad day. You can be hopeful in hopelessness, and you can overcome every obstacle that has hindered you mentally. It is possible and my hope is that I help you see this!

PANDEMIC

Recently I've found myself a little confused and falling back into old habits and negative patterns of thinking, trying so desperately to get back to my normal routine. Life can be so funny, changing without warning, so we don't even realize how fragile life can be. Our sense of normalcy can be snatched from us without even a chance to understand or accept it. The fact we have very little control when it comes to certain matters can be so frustrating. Many have come to understand this very fact of life in the recent pandemic and global crisis with Covid-19.

It just causes me to reconsider my approach to life, consider what is truly important with regards to suicide and depression. Issues like this just make an already bad situation worse. It's a scary thought to see things we often take for granted be slowly taken from us. For some people, things have been snatched away so quickly you can barely wrap your mind around what is happening. The truth is, it's a life-or-death situation, out of our present control. As the days pass by and things seemingly get worse, I wonder if my priorities were ever in the proper place. Everything going on causes me to reflect on my life.

I look at all the things I've overlooked, the things that seem so small and irrelevant. I didn't realize they were a gift. Life has new focus and new meaning, especially with all that is happening around us. We have a choice: to panic and be afraid, or to be positive and utilize all we have to make the most of this situation. It can be hard to be positive in the midst of so much negativity. The fact that everything is changing can be stressful, and it's difficult to see a silver lining.

Once I realized I needed to take a personal assessment to get a handle on everything that was happening around me, I began to see the bigger picture. Life has always been uncertain and it doesn't get easier to cope with reality, even without a pandemic. I can't just focus on what was lost, but I need to take the time to recognize what I've gained.

Covid-19, the global pandemic has affected everything: the way we shop, travel, communicate, and visit family and friends. It has affected the way we work. So many have lost their lives to this disease. Every day, the numbers go up while we wait for a possible cure. Sometimes I stop and look around at how everything has changed. Wearing a mask just to enter a store. The malls and movie theaters are losing business. So many stores and businesses have closed their doors. This is the new normal and it's depressing. Yet with all the negativity, I still feel hopeful, because I see this as an opportunity for the world to be more cautious, clean, productive, and mindful of each other. This is a time for us to spend time with our families, resolve emotional issues, and deal with things we've been avoiding.

This is an opportunity to build a relationship with God. A time of reflection on priorities that have been neglected. This is our opportunity to be grateful and thankful for our lives, our health, our families, and having things we need. Life is so unpredictable and fragile we must not take even a moment for granted. As I adjusted my outlook and attitude toward this pandemic and life in general, I realized if I don't utilize my gift to encourage and inspire others out of despair, it will be wasted. I want my experiences to be used to bless someone else who feels like giving up. I know how hard life is. This pain you're experiencing, you're not alone in it.

I understand how it feels to want the anxiety to stop, how you blame yourself and feel so defeated over every mistake and mishap in your life. I'm here to tell you no matter how far you have gone into depression, sadness, sin, heartbreak, loss, addiction, and suicidal thoughts, you can feel happy, experience joy, have peace of mind, be forgiven and forgive yourself.

Say this prayer:

Lord Jesus, I come to You as I am. Help me in the areas of my mind and heart that are full of fear, pain, and doubt. Comfort my mind. Bring peace and joy over me right now. Surround me with Your presence. Whatever is causing me to feel like giving up on life, bring restoration over me and help me to have positive, peaceful thoughts. Forgive me for all of my sins and help me to forgive myself. I choose to walk with You, Jesus, and I accept Your purpose for me. Help me to be all You created me to be. Let nothing I have experienced hold me back from Your love. Help me to have faith in all the areas where I have anxiety, fear, and doubt. I welcome You, Jesus, into my life. Destroy every negative thought that has kept me in bondage mentally. I receive freedom and joy right now. In Jesus' name. Amen.

Life is a process, but when you choose to walk with God, everything changes for the better. Jesus will turn your hopelessness to hope, your fear into faith, your tragedy into triumph, your pain into peace, and your hurt into joy. This is what Jesus has done for me. It takes courage to tell your story, but Jesus changed the direction of my entire life.

He was with me even in the mistakes I made, when I had doubt and wasn't faithful as I should have been. This is the reason I can tell my story without shame, because I didn't stay where the pain left me. I have seen the goodness of the Lord and it's real. My hope is that you will see the possibilities of your life walking with Jesus. I promise it's worth the journey!

YOUR LIFE MATTERS

Yes, you do matter. Your life matters. Your opinion matters. The things you care about matter. The things you need matter. Everything that makes you who you are matters! You can be courageous! You can get through whatever is trying to defeat you mentally or physically. You can make a difference. **You definitely have a purpose.**

I know the feeling of mental defeat. Wanting to give up in complete hopelessness. Friends and family telling you to just get up and get out of bed, just start your day, you'll get over it soon. Depression isn't that simple or easy to deal with. You feel like you're stuck. No matter how hard you try to be positive or uplifted, it seems to drag you down more and more each day. It leaves you lost, not knowing what to do. Constant negative thoughts race through your mind, dragging you down to the point of giving up on life, your future, and everything.

Do you feel as if your very existence is pointless? Well, I'm here to tell you that's a lie. I want to share my experiences with you, to uplift you and inspire you to keep pushing forward. Depression isn't easy for anyone, but you can defeat it and feel good about your life.

Be encouraged. You are not alone. I understand the pain and frustration of trying to go to school and work, keep a smile on your face for the world, while dying on the inside.

Nothing seems to go right, and even with small victories something else always would be wrong. I understand needing a break, and never able to get one.

I know how it feels to be bullied and no one cares. I know how it feels to be so overworked and overwhelmed with your entire life. I know how it feels to be stuck in bed, telling yourself to get up, but you don' t have the energy to move.

I want you to know life gets better. Some things aren't as bad as they seem. Some people are heartless and cruel, but just because they don't like you, that doesn't mean you are worthless. Sleep and a proper diet count so much, and prayer is everything.

When negative thoughts torment your mind, remember you are special and you do matter. Repeat it until it sinks in and you believe it, because it's true. Take the time to write ten things you like about yourself and your family. What are your unique talents and abilities? What makes you different and what kinds of things do you enjoy? What are your dreams and goals? All of these things are amazing qualities. Your life's purpose is in the things you love and struggle with the most.

YOU ARE AMAZING

Do you realize how unique you are? Do you know how completely different each person is from the next, your personalities, likes and dislikes?

Psalm 139:14 - *I praise you, because I am fearfully and wonderfully made; your works are wonderful.*

The human dynamic is so amazing and complex. You are incredible. Do you know that you, yes you, are completely amazing? You are so unique and different. Guess what? God *meant* you to be. You weren't made to fit in, but to stand out.

Most people who have the hardest time in life are those who are special and different. They feel like something is wrong with them, not realizing the very things that are unique about them are *supposed to be* unique. You have been blessed with the gift of change, meaning your purpose is about the very things that make you who you are. Did you know that God planted your dreams, gifts, and abilities within you?

This was purposefully done, and when you realize you can be everything God wants you to be by following His lead, it becomes possible. I know being young or just confused, it's hard to see yourself beyond the negative things people have called you. Sometimes your friends and family can be harsh with their criticism, not realizing they're breaking your heart. It can be difficult to feel like you have anything to offer with so much being called wrong, but consider what is right. Think about what is good. Even when it's hard to do so.

You're incredible and you have something to offer in this world. You were born for a reason, and when you take Jesus' hand and believe you can have a bright future, it becomes possible. He paid the cost to give you everything you need. That's how your ordinary can become extraordinary. So many people go through life feeling like there is no hope because they can't fit into society's box of perfection.

The truth is, no one was made to match this cookie cutter version of what a person should be. When I was ten years old. I started coming into my own and thinking about the kind of person I wanted to be. I've always been attracted to fashion and different patterns of clothing, taking pictures, being in front of the camera or center stage. Beauty and modeling were my passion and still are to this day.

My heart jumps for joy at the thought of a career in modeling. These days I've felt very humbled by my experiences and grateful for all the different opportunities I've had to model, internationally and in the United States. It was my dream and passion, and I'm so grateful to the Lord for allowing me to experience my dreams in that way.

It's very satisfying to have done something in your life that makes you happy and full of joy. I've come to realize that sometimes we can't always do what we want in life, but we can do what we enjoy and be a blessing to others. I'm still pursuing my modeling career. I'm hopeful that one day I'll be on the cover of my favorite magazine and modeling for a beautiful brand of clothing. Making a living out of doing something I love. And I also feel hopeful that if I can't have this come to reality for me, I will make it a reality every day in the way I treat others.

I will use my gifts and talents to encourage and inspire young people and others not to give up on themselves or their goals. I will use my gifts to bring change in the hearts of the hopeless and hurting by shining God's light through acts of kindness, generosity, encouragement, and compassion. I will walk in this world and let the streets be my runway, while I tell every kid, teenager, young adult or anyone struggling to find hope, "You are amazing, you deserve to be celebrated and you have purpose."

This is how to take life's lemons and make lemonade. Take what you can do and make something wonderful out of it. I encourage you today to ask Jesus to be your partner in life. Ask the Lord to lead you to your purpose, heal the pain in your heart, and make everything new.

Pray this simple prayer:

Lord Jesus, help me have a heart that follows You. Show me the way to go in life. Lead me to my purpose to help me to have understanding about myself and my unique life. Help me to have peace and heal me of every pain. In Jesus' name. Amen.

Stand out

ANXIETY AND MENTAL BATTLES

I remember when I was in the third grade. I was extremely shy and nervous. It was hard for me to talk and make eye contact, out of fear of being embarrassed or that I'd look stupid. I hated reading out loud. My voice would crack and tremble. The class would laugh, making all my insecurities even worse. We all know kids can be cruel and brutally honest at times, especially bullies, if they pick up on a weakness or something that really gets you down. They make it their business to ridicule you relentlessly over and over again, not allowing you to get a break. It somehow fuels them to see someone else defeated and hurt. Sad facts. I remember being asked by my teacher to read my poem aloud for the class. I think I stuttered over every word. I was shaking and my voice was cracking. I felt like I would pass out.

In my mind I kept saying, *I will mess up and everyone will laugh at me.* I cared way too much about what my classmates thought. The anxiety built up so bad, I could barely read through the first sentence. Of course, the other kids laughed at me and made jokes. I was so embarrassed and hurt, all I could do was cry. I felt so stupid, not knowing this kind of anxiety would follow me in different forms most of my life.

As I got older, it only got worse. My anxiety built up in almost every situation. Thoughts of: *I'm stupid. No one likes me. All they will do is laugh at me. I'm not important. No one cares. I'll fall and look dumb when I walk down the hall. Everyone is looking at me and thinks I'm ugly. I'm useless. I can't read in front of the class. I'm too shy. I'll just end up looking and feeling dumb. It's my fault. I'm so stupid. I'm such a fool. What's the point? I'm getting what I deserve. Nothing good is coming my way. I'm a joke, that's why everyone laughs at me. It's my fault he hurt me. It's my fault this happened. I will fail. I'm not where I'm supposed to be in life. Everyone hates me. I'll never be able to accomplish great things. I'm just worthless. Not good enough. Not pretty enough. My family doesn't care. I'm just in the way. I'm taking up space in the world. Everyone would be better off without me. No matter how hard I try, I'm not good enough. What's the point? I give up. I'm done. I'm just ugly and no one will love me. If I cared about that family member who died I would have been there more. I'm the reason why everything is messed up.*

If you have experienced any of these kinds of relentless thoughts racing through your mind constantly, you've experienced anxiety. This is so depressing for so many people around the world. It's a mental suffering that most don't understand unless they are going through it themselves.

For some, it's like your brain won't shut up with all the drama from your past, present, or your possible future. It's like being bullied, but you're the one throwing all the blows. It's not escaping yourself or things you have been through. Your mind constantly reminds you of each failure, each shortcoming, every unkind word, every situation that has left you hurt or broken, every time things didn't work out, every tragedy, every death or loss of a loved one or relationship, every fear, every doubt, every negative outcome. It's non-stop. Some people can barely sleep or have a productive day without being overwhelmed and bombarded with all the mental anguish.

Some people resort to finding an escape that shuts off the negative thoughts. Some try drinking, drugs, food, smoking, medication, natural remedies, prayer or talking to a counselor.

Escaping from anxiety through drugs and drinking only causes more problems, because it only gives an illusion of the problem being fixed. Actually, it's only masking the problem and inadvertently becoming another problem altogether.

Personally, I've always hated drugs and alcohol, because I've seen friends and family destroyed from the effects. When I turned twenty-three years old, I started researching how to face my fears and the root cause of my anxiety. I had to be honest with myself. I had to be honest about my past, my experiences, my childhood, my negative thought patterns, my self-esteem, the pressures I faced, and things that happened that were out of my control.

My discovery was amazing and it helped me with my anxiety. I got really honest with myself and I realized how many things I felt and believed stemmed from experiences when I was young and things I went through as I got older. I had stuffed so much of my pain and fears into the back of my mind, hoping to just be able to move on with my life without actually healing from these experiences.

I was suppressing my pain and my problems by letting things build up, and not addressing them. I tried to pretend it never happened or I wasn't affected by it. Whenever I felt at fault for something in my life, I'd beat myself up over it, convinced that was what I deserved for allowing certain things to happen. So all through my life, these anxious thoughts popped in and out of my mind, reminding me of things I'd rather not deal with or just hoped to forget.

These thoughts affected my life in numerous ways. I couldn't get proper sleep, I couldn't focus on goals, or needed transitions in my life. I couldn't effectively accomplish anything, because I felt like I'd only fail. I had no peace or real joy, just living life on a moment-by-moment basis. I wore a fake smile, to cover up mentally being tortured by negative feelings and thoughts.

Sometimes I'd get so overwhelmed from suppressing everything, I'd have panic attacks. I could barely breathe. No one should live life in this much pain and suffering. It's a sad reality for so many people, suffering in silence with anxiety and depression.

The first step I took in recovering from my anxiety was taking the time to be real with myself and my emotions. I took time to confront myself in my thoughts without running from the feelings or negativity. I asked myself what was the problem? Why do I feel this way? What started me feeling this way or having these thoughts? I wrote everything down. How I felt about myself and why. How I felt about my life experiences. Break-ups. Losing a loved one to death. How I felt about my overall life and areas I wanted to improve and why I felt I couldn't change. How others have affected my life and how they have affected my self-esteem. As I wrote down all of these questions and began to answer them, I realized so much of my pain came from unforgiveness. I had been wrong in many ways throughout my life. Some of the blame for my mistakes and failures and misery were on me, and I overly disappointed myself by being too concerned with how the world viewed me.

Most of my mental anguish was because I had not forgiven myself or others. My time in God's word allowed me to get validation and confidence in who God created me to be, and to learn to only be concerned with His view of my life and who I am as a person. I spent time learning about forgiveness and the benefits of releasing the pain and hurts of the past to Jesus, instead of trying to harbor all of it in my heart and mind. I realized the importance of forgiving others and also forgiving myself for the negative role I've played in my life experiences.

The most important realization I made about my anxiety was that because I had unforgiveness in my heart toward myself and others, this had given demonic spirits free reign to use my past against me, replaying negative thoughts and experiences in my life over and over again.

In return, I accepted these negative thoughts about myself and my circumstance, because I believed these thoughts to be my own. I felt as if I deserved nothing but mental anguish because I wasn't perfect. I realized my mind was under attack from an evil demonic force that was (trying to steal my peace and joy) Even though I had moved on from my past, my mind wouldn't allow me to move past it until I surrendered all my pain and hurt to the Lord.

I realized God had given me free will to choose. Unknowingly, I was choosing to not forgive, trying to deal with my pain and problems on my own. When we leave room for the enemy to come into our lives by trying to handle everything in our lives separated from God, the devil sees this as an opportunity to strike against you and battle your mind.

You must choose, saying: *Lord Jesus, I want to forgive others. I want to be healed of my life experiences. I want to grow in the areas I'm weak. I want Your protection from the enemy over my mind and my body. I choose life and peace.*

Until you make that conscious decision, you will continue to be plagued by negative thoughts and emotions.

If you are ready to be guilt-free, at peace, forgiven of your sins, walking in victory and starting a journey in life that is new and exciting, full of purpose, full of happiness and mercy, and free from mental bondage, pray this simple prayer:

Lord Jesus, I believe You died on the cross for my sins and You rose again on the third day so that I too will be resurrected and spend eternity in heaven. I receive Your free gift of salvation through faith in You, and I ask You to help me to forgive others as well as myself for all the things I've done wrong and wrongs done against me.

I repent of my sins. I ask You to heal my heart and my mind and allow my sleep to be peaceful and my days to be full of joy. Bless me to see myself as You see me, and help me not be concerned with the ways of the world. Mold my heart to do Your plans and bless others. In Jesus' name. Amen.

Your life matters, and nothing can stop you from having a blessed life. You are amazing and you can accomplish great things. Just believe.

OPPOSITION

Life can be cruel, and living with depression doesn't make it any easier. Finding balance between work and school can be almost impossible. What really gets difficult is trying to pretend around family and friends that you're fine when really, you're not. Personally, I hate when people fuss over me. So dramatic and over the top. Sometimes you just want to deal with your depression in your own way. The fact is, when your depression is out of control and you feel hopeless to the point of suicide, you actually need someone to make a big deal about it. In my experience, I felt like it was burdensome to say anything about my feelings, for fear of being misunderstood.

What I've realized is that hiding my depression only made things worse for me. No one knew I was suffering, so how could they help? At times it's fine to be independent and handle our own emotional baggage. It is also important to know when to admit to ourselves we need help. Making everyone play a guessing game to figure out something is wrong only hurts you in the long run. Don't ever suffer in silence. No one is a mind reader, and if we don't speak up about what we are dealing with, how can we expect to heal or be helped? Some battles can only be won with other people lending a hand.

I definitely get it. I've been there too many times, locked away, isolated from the world. I wanted to be alone, but at the same time I wanted help. I couldn't bring myself to ask for it because I felt like I would look foolish or not be taken seriously. Basically, I had too much pride. So I sank into myself and just slowly died inside.

It's a hopeless feeling. Sometimes I didn't even know what was wrong or why I was feeling so low and defeated. At times, life would just throw that last sucker punch and it would take me down. I had to realize my hurt stemmed from multiple areas of pain, hurt, disappointments, thoughts, and emotions. I was overwhelmed with reluctance and stressed out from not being where I needed to be.

Sometimes I couldn't pinpoint exactly why I was so depressed. It would seem as if everything hit me all at once. Old pains would resurface, new struggles would emerge. It didn't take much to tip the scale of my agony, because everything I had suppressed was building up and overflowing. It felt like I was ready to burst out of the seams of my emotions at any given moment.

It's a heavy burden to bear all of your past and your present on your shoulders without catching your breath, to give yourself any relief or peace. I don't think in my struggles with depression I ever had much peace. I had more days of pretending to be happy or trying to make myself happy, but still so dissatisfied with myself and life.

So what exactly is peace? Is it having everything you ever wanted? Is it not having any hardships? Is peace having a love life? Is it getting a dream job? Is peace having popularity? Is peace perfection? Is peace having enough money?

In definition peace is freedom from disturbance; tranquility. A state or period in which there is no war, or a war has ended. In today's world, we rarely can have a moment of tranquility. Freedom from disturbance is next to impossible, with all the outside demands and everyday pressures. Our lack of proper rest is definitely catching up with us and affecting our emotional state of mind.

Then there are times when we are at war within ourselves. A war that seems to never end, because there is always something else being thrown on our emotional plates to deal with. The truth is our peace is constantly disrupted. Our levels of happiness fluctuate. Our emotions can be all over the place, experiencing extreme highs, and in the next moment extreme lows. It's difficult to stay positive when there is so much negativity surrounding you.

It makes you wonder if it is really possible to get through difficult times. Is it possible to have peace and happiness even when everything around you is going wrong? Do we just pretend? Do we just fake it until we make it? Is there any resolution to cope with these issues? Can you be happy even though nothing is going right? Is there any hope? The truth is, life won't let up on you, and this world won't either. There will always be an obstacle to hurdle over. And there will be more pain and disappointment. Life will always have its ups and downs. We are all aware of this.

The real mystery is how we get back up after falling and remain resilient, motivated, strong, healthy, persevering, and relentless.

Personally, I like to take the comic book approach. Imagine you're a hero in an action movie like Captain Marvel or Superman, and the villain is whatever obstacle you are facing today. You might be facing hopelessness, sickness, failure, pain, heart break, bullies, negative thoughts, financial problems, loneliness, fear, guilt, trauma, anxiety, peer pressure, abuse, addiction, or suicidal thoughts. Anything that has weighed you down mentally and exerted your energy and self-esteem.

These things are the villains in your life that are robbing you of joy and peace. Imagine yourself as strong as your favorite superhero. Yet you have this advantage you're not aware of yet. You're actually invincible against the opposition, your "kryptonite," your weakness is only an illusion created by the villains in your mind. It is only an illusion that you are not strong enough to overcome your problems, that you are weak. The villains (strongholds) in your life have used trickery to con your mind into believing you can't win. Yet you are more than what you even realize. The devil uses your obstacles against you to make you feel overwhelmed. He is a villain, an enemy after our peace, joy and our very souls.

The truth is this villain is no match for you, when you choose Jesus. Imagine having this power source where you're unlimited in what you can do, and you are more powerful than you even realize. Imagine the power source is your heart, God's love for you. This power source is ignited through faith. Think of all your goals, love, dreams, friends, family, parents, grandparents, that childhood cartoon, your favorite show, favorite time of the year, anything that makes you smile, your favorite movies, jokes that make you laugh, your favorite food, things that touched your heart, people who showed you incredible kindness, moments in your life that left you on a natural high, all your memories of victory, all your wins in life.

That's your weapon of positivity. Imagine using that as fuel for a force field to explode the chains of mental bondage and break free. Imagine being bold and courageous, fearless against all the hurt and all the pain in your life. You are untouchable, but you didn't realize it until now. Imagine knocking down each villain that has mentally put you in a corner, and saying, "I am strong. I can get through this. I've come too far to give up now. I will fight for my life and you have no power over me." Imagine facing everything that worried you and defeated you and realizing you're invincible. This kind of strength comes from laying every burden in your life at the cross. Giving over every stress and problem to Jesus. Having faith He will restore you and bless you.

Imagine getting up out of that dark corner and standing on your feet, radiating bright light all around you. You are so powerful, all of the issues (villains) have turned to dust, and now you realize you were in control all along! You walk out of the prison where you were mentally held captive and you set others free.

You are the hero in your own life the moment you realize your life is worth fighting for. If you feel like you have no more fight left in you, tag a friend to help. Depression battles are real, but you have the power. Stand up and say, "Enough," and make a decision to get help, once you realize you have come too far to give up now. Jesus has given me the courage to keep going even when I felt like dying was my only option. The Lord gave me the strength to live! You can have that same strength by putting your faith in God's ability.

A FATHER'S BETRAYAL

Fathers are so important in a kid's life. I can only imagine how different life would be if I had a father in my life who contributed to my development. I actually met my father for the first time when I was seventeen years old. I didn't know a lot about him, other than he was my father. So, I was curious to meet him and I wondered where he was most of my life. I was seventeen and my daughter was one year old at the time.

I need to discuss how this happened, before I talk about the harm done by not having a father in my life.

I was sexually assaulted by a man who told me he was much younger than his actual age. Everything I knew about him was a lie. I met him on a city bus. I was fifteen at the time. He asked me my name and age. I told him I was fifteen and I asked him how old he was. He said seventeen and I believed him. I gave him my number and we talked on the phone. He seemed nice. He was very tall, six-feet-four-inches. I was barely five-foot-two at the time. He asked me over to his house to hang out. He said we could watch a movie and eat pizza, and his grandmother didn't mind us hanging out in the living room. I told him, yeah sure. I'd ask my grandma if she could bring me over. I knew if I told my grandmother I was going to a boy's house, she probably wouldn't take me. So I unfortunately lied and said I was visiting a girl from school.

My grandmother dropped me off and I told her to pick me up in a few hours, because we were going to watch a movie and eat pizza. I went and knocked on the door and he answered. I was really happy to see him and was looking forward to talking and watching a movie. I noticed when I came in that we were all alone. I was confused. I thought his grandmother was home. I was expecting to meet her. I asked where his grandmother was and he said she was at a bingo game and wouldn't be back for a while.

I felt a little uneasy, but I thought it was fine. He didn't have any movies or pizza. He sat down on the couch next to me and he touched my thigh and said I looked pretty. He then kissed me. I didn't really want to move that fast. We hadn't even held hands yet or got to know each other much at all. He kissed me more aggressively and started to move in closer and closer, pulling my legs to force me to lie on the couch. I told him to wait and to not do that, but he wouldn't listen.

My heart raced and I didn't know what to do. He was so heavy and I wasn't strong enough to push him away. I told him to stop, I'd never gone this far before and I didn't think we should. I was not ready yet. He kept touching me and pulling up my shirt. I told him to stop and he was hurting me, but he wouldn't listen. He kept saying I wanted him. I must have, because I came all the way over there and I wore a skirt. I only came over to hang out and watch movies and talk, maybe one kiss, but I wasn't trying to go that far. I struggled back and forth with him until he overpowered me. He pulled up my skirt and jerked off my underwear.

I felt so helpless and afraid. This wasn't anything like the cute teenage movies I'd watch and imagine having my first kiss. I just wanted to hold hands and talk and laugh, maybe play a game, eat pizza, and plan our next get together. I struggled with him, trying to pull my skirt back down into place, while he used one hand to hold me down and the other to unzip his pants.

All in that moment, I regretted lying to my grandmother and wearing the skirt and trusting him. I felt so stupid and so ugly. I kept thinking this was my fault. I lied. I shouldn't have lied. I shouldn't have come over there. Why did he do this to me? I thought he liked me. Why would he hurt me like this? It was all my fault. I did something to deserve this. After he sexually assaulted me at his grandmother's house, he acted as if it was a normal thing, like it was okay. My arms hurt, my legs hurt, everything hurt from struggling to try to stop him. I had bruises and I felt like dying.

My grandmother arrived and blew the car horn to let me know she was outside. I ran to the car and I tried to act normal. As soon as I got home, I went in my room and just cried this hopeless cry. I didn't tell my grandmother or my mother, because I felt like it was my fault. I lied about who I was seeing. I felt like there was nothing I could do. At the time I wasn't familiar with the terms *rape* or *sexual assault*. I knew nothing about sex, other than sex education in school, and I had no idea that I was a victim of a crime even though I came over to see him. When I talked to him on the phone, we hadn't talked about sex, and I naively thought we would really watch movies and eat pizza. I kept it secret and just tried to pretend it didn't happen. Months went by and I just tried to avoid the issue about what I went through with him.

He'd call and I'd answer the phone. He still acted as if everything was okay. I was so hurt by everything, and it was weighing heavy on me. I wasn't doing that great in school. I usually got an A-B honor roll, but I wasn't motivated to study or care about my class work. I tried really hard to pretend I was okay. He called me one day while my grandmother was out of town and talked me into letting him come over. That was a huge mistake. He said he was sorry about how things went at his house and he wanted to see me in person to say he was sorry.

I believed him and told him I was home alone. He came over and said he was sorry, only to push up on me and take advantage of me a second time. I found out later he wasn't seventeen. He was an adult.

Months went by and I was throwing up and extremely tired all the time. I had no idea why. My only thought was maybe I was sick with the stomach flu, like I had when I was thirteen in middle school. My mom asked me when was my last period and if I was having sex. She said, "You have symptoms of pregnancy." I broke down and told her everything. I didn't think once that I was pregnant. At fifteen I didn't have a clue about too much of anything, and it was sad how easily I got caught up in that situation. My biggest regret was not listening to my mom and my grandmother.

As a kid, you want to have fun and have those cute experiences you see in teen movies. I had no idea that real life doesn't work that way. I valued my mother's words more after that experience.

Having a period was fairly new to me, and now my period was late. I still was getting used to having a period, so *not* having one didn't mean anything to me. I hadn't been having them long enough to know the difference. It was a mess. I was an emotional wreck, young and so clueless about everything. We went to the doctor and I found out I was six months pregnant.

My belly wasn't very big at all. I had suffered all my morning sickness and fatigue, thinking I was just going through the stomach flu again. It was scary, finding out I was pregnant with a little tiny baby growing inside me and I'd be a mom in less than three months. It was heart-wrenching to realize I was sexually assaulted, lied to, and manipulated by a grown man who knew I was only fifteen. I still felt like it was my fault. He even knew this and took advantage of the fact I didn't fully understand what was going on. I felt so dumb and stupid. My mom explained to me that it wasn't right how he treated me, even though I lied and went to see him. Having sex should have been a choice, not forced on me, overpowered by his physical strength. She said I should have told them immediately, and even though I would have been in trouble, it wasn't worth suffering like that alone. She was right. It's heartbreaking how cruel people can be, and it's so sad when kids are hurt by adults who are fully aware of what they are doing.

I had my daughter, and she was such a blessing. She's my little sunshine and I see her as my inspiration and hope because she grew up with me and we have such an amazing relationship. It's unfortunate how things happened, but she was the blessing and the good out of the negativity, so I was always grateful and thankful for her. My daughter knows about who her father is. It bothers her that he hurt me in that way. He tried to hurt me again when I was nineteen. The courts gave him a permanent restraining order for me and my daughter, because they said he was unfit to be around me or any child.

When I was in high school, he stalked me at school and tried to keep bullying me. My mother suggested I go to the Job Corps to get away from him and all the stress. So I went to Job Corp to finish high school in Charleston, West Virginia. I completed everything and earned college credits in six months, at seventeen going on eighteen. It was nice to get away from all the harassment, even though I missed my daughter and my family so much.

I carried that pain for years. It was definitely a depressing situation that caused so much pain in my life. It took a while to heal from that. I had to forgive myself for not being honest with my grandmother and holding that secret from my mom.

I had to look at what happened and forgive the man who hurt me, and I had to look at my daughter and see everything was okay, and even though she didn't have a father, she had me and I'd love her and protect her always, and try my best to be open with her so she wouldn't be naive about her body or men.

I wanted something different and better for her. So I met my father at seventeen years old. I really didn't have many details about who he was or why he wasn't in my life. As time went on, I discovered there was something about him that wasn't right. I found out my mother had me at the age of fourteen and my father was almost forty at the time. My mother and his oldest daughter used to go to school together. My mother was a very young child and my father was an adult, a union that wasn't supposed to be. I learned he had been in prison for fifteen years for shooting a woman to death in front of her two young children. This man was a murderer and pedophile. This created so much conflict in me. How could this man smile in my face and pretend everything was just normal or okay?

I saw him a few times and I didn't know exactly how to feel about myself, or about knowing what happened to my mother. I was the result of that. It broke my heart. A part of me wished I never knew these details. I felt hurt, ashamed, and just confused. I remember crying and asking God: Why do these types of things happen to people, to children? How do we get past this pain? It's too much to bear. It's heartbreaking. It's horrible to know your very existence came from just a horrible crime against a child.

At fourteen, you're just starting high school, possibly still sleeping with a favorite teddy bear. You're just starting puberty and trying to cope with all the physical changes, watching cartoons, eating your favorite cereal, and roller skating at the park. At fourteen, you still need to grow up yourself, but you're becoming a mother. How can a man bring himself to want a child in a way that no child should be looked at? To steal a child's innocence and betray her in that way. How could he steal her youth, her childhood, and not care about the consequences? Adults are supposed to guide, protect and teach children. A good man would have never done this.

My conclusion was that my father wasn't a good man. Realizing how much had been taken from my mother, I just felt sorry for being born. I wished I could have protected her from him. I wished I could do something to make everything right. My mother deserved better than that. She may have not been his child, but she was someone's child. He had a daughter around my mother's age. I wondered how he could look at her and not see his own daughter.

I could never understand the mindset of a person who would look at a young child in this way. It's heartbreaking and extremely horrible. So many people live with these heart-wrenching secrets, pains, and things no one speaks of. So many families have issues like this or worse, and they just pretend it never happened. Just keep living, just keep smiling, just keep going like this elephant in the room isn't there.

It's a hurt that leaves scars for a lifetime, and hiding or keeping secrets only creates deeper wounds that lead to addictions, which only suppress the pain but never alleviate it. I vowed to my mother to honor her and love her and protect her and do anything I could for her for the rest of her life. My mother is a diamond. Her heart is golden and her love is timeless. Her perseverance, her strength and her love are so amazing. What she went through was meant to destroy her and to destroy me, but God had different plans.

Truly He turned around the worst evil and allowed good to come out of it. I am nothing like my father. I forgive him, because I refuse to stop the blessing and the calling God has on my life. It's incredible what God can do when you look at what can be gained instead of what was lost.

I remember at nineteen years old, meeting my sister, Brenda. She was eighteen years old and she came to the area to live with our father. I later found out the woman my father killed was her mother. She was in school to be a nurse and was getting ready to graduate when our father decided one day to come into her home and shoot her in front of Brenda and her brother. My sister was only three and her brother was only six at the time. My sister told me he shot her mother in front of them and just walked out. She told me she remembered this and it scared her brother for life. It broke his heart and he lived with so much pain because of that incident. Her brother had to call 911 after our father left their mother there on the floor, dying. Brenda told me she came to live with our father because things were difficult and she had nowhere else to go.

During this time, I had only visited with my father a few times. I tried my best not to be angry and hold a grudge. I was trying to get to know my father's side of the family and just be positive. It's a difficult thing to try to block out the sad reality of what a person is and hope they have possibly changed. A part of me was curious about my family, because I wanted to know who I was, where my looks came from, and just be loved. My hopes were soon disrupted by the sad reality of who my father continued to be.

When I was nineteen years old, I worked for a construction company as a secretary. I wasn't making much money, but it was a decent job for me at that time. I had saved up about $600 and I needed a car. My father said he would help me get a vehicle and he took my money and found me a used 1994 Ford station wagon, which was fairly cheap. It was fine, it ran okay, but had a lot of mechanical problems. I asked my father to help with my insurance and he added me to the auto insurance policy. I paid him $125 a month for insurance. I didn't know any better at the time that liability coverage shouldn't have cost me that much. My father would come visit me at work and introduce himself as my father. He told my employers he painted vehicles for a living and asked if they were interested in his services.

He took money for the work on these vehicles from multiple people on my job. I found out months later he had primed the vehicles, which is removing all the old paint and buffing out the dents. He only stripped off the old paint, but never actually painted the vehicles the new paint he had promised. That put so much stress on me, because my boss and the other staff complained how my father took their money but never completed the job. My per-week wage was barely $100, and paying $125 a month took a big chunk out of my pay.

So I decided to call the insurance company to see if it was possible to get cheaper rates or if there were other insurance companies that could give me a cheaper policy. I first called the insurance my father had me under, and I learned he had four vehicles on this policy, including mine. The total cost for all four vehicles amounted to $150. I was very confused. He had me paying the bulk of the bill and he knew I wasn't making much money on my job. I had expenses and responsibilities. I had my daughter and rent. I called other auto insurance companies to get quoted insurance rates and found a policy that was so much cheaper than what I was paying my dad every month.

He was very upset that I called the insurance company and found out. A man who had not been in my life to care for me or assist in any way was taking from me instead of being there for me. He was looking out for his own best interests instead of mine. The tension got so bad on my job, I had to leave. My boss was so disappointed that my father cheated them, and they assumed I was the same way. So I lost my job. I will never forget how my boss said, "You're probably a con artist just like your dad." I never told my boss that I had just met him a year ago and I had no idea he would take their money and not complete the job he promised.

The more time went on, the more things about my father's character were revealed. I found out later my father was telling lies about me. He said he had brought me a car, he said he was paying for my car insurance, and he was doing things for me that he never did. The only thing my mom ever really got from him was a $100 check he had given her when I met him at the age of seventeen. I found out from my sister Brenda that so much more was going on. It was unfortunate that our father wasn't someone we could trust.

One night, I got a phone call from my sister, and she had told me our father took the money left for her from her mother's life insurance. He made promises he didn't keep concerning the money. He would get drunk and go to strip bars and come back and harass her for sex. He even went so far to say he had sex with me and tried to persuade her to have sex with him, based on this very twisted lie. She tried to tell the police what was going on, but he would manipulate the police by saying she was an out of control teen and she was making wild accusations because she couldn't have her way.

My sister was so outraged by the police not believing her, she tried to go to homeless shelters to get away from our father. He contacted every shelter in the area, saying she was a runaway and she was telling wild stories about him. She got in a cab, trying to find somewhere to go, and told the cab driver what was happening. He offered her help. I had no idea all of this was going on. After I got off the phone with my sister, I called my father immediately. I was very upset.

I said, "Wasn't it horrific enough you killed her mother? But you went so far as to actually try to make her have sex with you. Isn't it enough that you have stolen her chance of having her mother, but you want to take her entire will to live by trying to have sex with her? This is so beyond evil."

His only response was, "I did my time for that, I spent fifteen years in prison."

It broke my heart into a million pieces, because my sister was alone in this world without her mother and our father was a monster, portraying himself as someone with good intentions and motives. I'd sit back sometimes, wondering why this man was my father. Why did we have to be brought into this world in such a cruel way and discover this truth and live with it every day? How can a man be this heartless to his children and this cruel to our mothers?

He took my mother's childhood and her future. Her entire life was altered because of his evil, selfish decision to look at her in a way no child should be viewed. He took Brenda's mom's very life. He murdered her in cold blood in front of my sister and her brother. They had to figure out how to call the police. I hurt for every mother, child and person affected by rape, incest, and murder. One could ask: Is it even possible to heal from this or even be positive and forgiving?

I have chosen to forgive my father, because through Christ Jesus I have found peace. A peace that heals hurts that seems to never go away. My heart breaks thinking about it, but my heart now rejoices in the blessing of today, the present moment of what has been gained. My mother is courageous and strong, and I am so thankful she loved me despite the circumstances involving my birth. She has never given up on me and she has given me strength to persevere through the situations I've experienced with my daughter's father. She has given me the inspiration to be more than what people expect of me, and to realize there is hope. I recognized the blessing of having my sister in my life, and how we have become more than family, but best friends. I realized that God can take the worst tragedy and turn it into triumph. We have each other. We encourage each other, and sharing our stories has brought peace and healing to us.

I'm so thankful for my sister and I'm so proud of her courage and her amazing strength. We have hope even in the midst of our pain. I pray for my father, for him to change, to give his life to the Lord, and my hope is that he realizes the pain and destruction he has caused and makes efforts to make amends. This kind of hope that dwells within my mother, my daughter, my sister and me is the hope that only Jesus can give. He is healing us and renewing us daily. We are not victims but victorious in the everlasting grace that Jesus has given us to thrive in life and make a difference.

BUT THE LORD WAS WITH ME!

My testimony of God's grace in my life and His deliverance is that God has always been with me my entire life. I can look back and see God's hand in every area of my life, even when I was unaware of His presence.

When I was three years old and I was trying to get a glass out of the freezer, the glass broke and cut all my fingers on my right hand, requiring me to be in a cast for six months because my index finger was almost completely severed, but the Lord was with me.

When I was eight, I had a bike my cousin fixed for me, but the brakes didn't work so well. I hit a tree and the bike's handlebars bike turned vertically and stabbed me in the stomach. I fell off the bike. I woke up in the hospital with a ruptured spleen, but the Lord was with me.

At ten years old, I was crossing the street to go to the recreation center. My brother ran ahead of me. I tried to catch up. I got to the intersection of the street and a car was coming so fast, I stopped in the middle of the street to let the car pass. I started to back up, but the car sped up even faster and even slightly turned and hit me. I remember being hit so hard I was thrown in the air and my shoes fell off my feet. While I was in the air, I felt something catch me and gently lay me on the ground. I had no bruises or broken bones. The Lord was with me.

I remember when I was twelve years old, I was playing outside. Another kid was playing with his brother. He had a metal seat he threw like a Frisbee, trying to hit his little brother, but it hit me in the face, knocking out a front tooth and cutting my lip. My mother rushed me to the emergency room. I got stitches. The doctor told us if it wasn't for my severely crooked teeth, I would have lost all of my teeth in the front and possibly could have died. But the Lord was with me.

I remember being fifteen, and needing to go use a pay phone in the neighborhood. We couldn't afford a regular house phone and I wanted to call my cousin and a few friends of mine. My mom told me not to go outside after dark, and especially late like after 10:00pm. Being fifteen and rebellious. I went outside anyway thinking I could go and nothing bad would happen. At this point, I was eight-and-a-half months pregnant. I had been on the pay phone for about fifteen minutes when this car drove by. The next thing I knew, I was hearing gunshots

I don't know if they were aiming at me or the people across the street or what was going on, but something in (my) mind told me to run. I dropped the pay phone and I ran as fast as I could. I got shot through the back of my thigh and upper hip area. No bones or major arteries were hit. My mother drove me to the hospital. The next day I saw the phone booth was completely covered in bullet holes. If I didn't run when I did, I probably wouldn't be here today. I was okay because the Lord was with me.

I remember waking up, nine months pregnant, with really bad pains in my back. I told my mom how bad my back was hurting, and she said it might be labor. We got to the hospital, and within thirty minutes of arriving, I had given birth to my daughter. There was no time for an epidural or any kind of pain medicine, because I was already so many centimeters dilated. I had basically slept through my contractions. By the grace of God, I didn't go through a lot of pain. I was okay, because the Lord was with me.

Life has been incredibly difficult for me, but I remember when I was about seven years old and my great-grandmother was talking to me about Jesus. I believed at that moment. I didn't quite understand what it all meant, but the seed was planted in my heart, and as I grew older, my relationship with Jesus only became stronger.

I went to college and got a degree in business. Things still were very difficult for me. I got married at nineteen and that didn't work out. I didn't want to drop out of college and I needed to support myself and my daughter. My husband had suggested I go to school full time, because his military allotment would be enough to take care of the bills. So I left my job at the construction company where I was a secretary. My husband was sleeping with other women and had another apartment in his name that he shared with someone else. He got another girl pregnant and left me and my daughter. I didn't have a job and I was enrolled in college full time. It was too late to change my class schedule back to part-time. I was so close to finishing school. I didn't know what to do. I thought my marriage was going to last. I trusted my husband, but now I believe he really just wanted the extra dependent money from the military to do his own thing. We eventually got a divorce and realized we were better off friends.

So, I decided to dance at a Go-Go bar, to make enough money to take care of my daughter and stay in school. People would judge me and think I was just like everyone else there. I definitely understood their assumptions, the fact still remained that I worked there. I never thought of myself as better than any of the girls, just because I didn't take advances or sleep with men for money or drink alcohol or do drugs, but I was there just like them, trying to make money, trying to survive, broken and hurt. I didn't want to be there. So young and confused I didn't know what else to do at the time. I felt really bad for the girls and myself. It hurts to feel so unwanted and unworthy of better circumstances. I constantly prayed for them and myself, because I knew that prayer could change things. Most of the changes for me were happening in my heart and my spirit. I knew as I grew in God's word and understanding of my faith. One day I'd be able to have a better life.

Every girl there had a story and most people never cared enough to listen or help. The world we live in has very few outlets for women who have been victimized by rape, molestation and sexual assault. It's a sad reality how so many women are taken advantage of mentally, physically, sexually and emotionally. Leaving us with very few options to survive. Someone who hasn't walked in these womens shoes assumes they are just full of greed or sexual immorality when most of them are battling pain and problems no one even knows about. Some use that lifestyle as a way to escape or numb the pain of their past.

Even while I was there, people would have conversations with me. I still would talk about Jesus and they would be confused. Like: "How can you be in this place and still talk about God and still talk about the Bible?" One thing I realized about God is that He accepts you right where you are. Even if you're stuck or if you're in a situation or you're struggling in some area of your life, Jesus has mercy for you that the world doesn't.

I realized if we don't allow Jesus to deal with our hearts, we won't have the power to do right by ourselves. We need Him to give us the grace to do His will. We need the Holy Spirit to lead us and guide us. Even in that situation, He was dealing with me about my self-esteem, my self-worth, my pain, and my broken heart from everything I had experienced. It's amazing how much Jesus loves us. Even in that situation, He was working on me. That environment couldn't stop what Jesus was doing inside my heart and spirit.

I'm still progressing in my faith, it's very humbling how God has given me insight and compassion for people through my experiences. God can use what was meant to destroy you as a testimony to help others out of sin. The Lord is refining me and polishing me every day. Jesus can and will do the same for you, right where you are, no matter how deep you have fallen into sin. Jesus can restore you, heal you, and give you hope and a future.

PAIN AND SUICIDAL THOUGHTS

I had a thought during a time when I was very depressed, full of anxiety, stressed out, overwhelmed, overworked and just completely exhausted with life. I thought: *If I were to die today, would I be pleased with my life? Would I have regrets or unfinished things I want to accomplish? Would I be satisfied with the person I have become? Did I have unforgiveness toward someone who hurt me? Would I be angry with someone from my past? If I passed away today, would my life have been fulfilling or have purpose? Did I tell my loved ones I loved them, or did I accomplish anything rewarding? Was I consumed with being popular, following trends, trying to get all the money? Did my life have meaning? Did my existence help anyone else? Was my existence all about material gain or having a relationship or competing with someone else? Was my existence all about having fun, being careless, and feeling invincible?*

When I sat back and thought about all these questions I asked myself, I realized a lot of things in my life I was prioritizing as so important really weren't.

When I was sixteen, being popular, having a really nice car, having a lot of money, traveling, having the latest fashion, shoes, clothes and make-up were the things I wanted. These were my goals, but I was young. It's okay to be young and it is okay to want to have material things, but there's a difference between having things and things having you, which means making material things a higher priority over things that money can't buy. Money and possessions can't love us back. Chasing things instead reaching for depth in life is an empty pursuit, something I realized much later in life. I was so depressed and suicidal when I was very young, and it wasn't because I didn't have material things or a lot of money. It was a combination of circumstances, things that had happened to me, hopelessness, poverty and just feeling I was coming in last in everything. Other kids picking at me didn't help, so I was just feeling so unimportant, having low self-esteem, and not really knowing where I belonged or fit in.

I always felt awkward and out of place no matter where I was, even sometimes among family. I felt out of place and awkward, so different, when I wanted to be the same as everyone else. I didn't want to stand out so much or be ignored. I thought about the questions: *If I died today, can I honestly say as I left this earth I would be happy with my choices? Did I reach out for help, did I do everything possible in my life to make things better? Was I stubborn or full of pride? Would taking my life break my family's heart?*

I always hated talking about death, because I didn't want to imagine my life without anyone who was close to me, and I didn't want to even think about having to grieve their loss. It's a pain that can't be healed, an aching that still hurts no matter how much you get over it. Death is a scary thing. People pass away every day from illnesses, accidents and bad things that are out of their control, but suicide is a choice a person is in control of.

At its foundation is a scary, heart-wrenching, heart-breaking, emotional mental exhaustion of life that consumes people to the point they feel like it's unbearable to go on. Honestly, so many people are so exhausted and tired of being broken down mentally, to where they feel like death is their only escape. I know the feeling, but honestly, I didn't want to die. I just wanted the pain to stop. I just wanted the thoughts to stop. I just wanted the anxiety to stop. I just wanted to feel better and be okay.

The first step to my healing from depression and suicidal thoughts was when I realized I didn't want to break my mother's heart, or my brother's and sister's hearts. Or my daughter's heart, or friends who really loved me. I remember anxious thoughts, like: *Nobody cares about me. The world would be better without me anyway. It's pointless, my entire life is pointless and everything in it is a joke. I would do my family and friends a favor by just leaving, just dying.* The same thoughts would come over me when I had a bad break-up, lost a job, or when someone would mistreat me or talk bad about me or put me down. Then there were the things that happened to me. The rape. All the bullying. Being a teenage parent. Not having many friends. Feeling like all my dreams were out of my reach and impossible. Being betrayed by people I trusted. Having to dance just to feed my child, when jobs wouldn't hire me. I thought: *If I took my life by choice, would it really make everything better? Would it really make everything okay? Would my pain really stop?*

Death seemed like the best option, but I knew I couldn't guarantee any of my pain would completely stop, even in death. I knew nothing about death other than it was the means to end life on earth. Not knowing exactly what to expect in death scared me as well. I had to really reflect on myself and question everything hurting me, everything bothering me, and everything contributing to me feeling this way.

I made the decision to fight. I realized that no matter how hard life had knocked me down, I still had a choice, and whatever came against me mentally, I wanted to overcome it. **Once you make up your mind to fight, everything in you goes into action against giving up.**

So, in my most difficult moment of despair, I decided to get a notebook, a cup of green tea with honey, and a pen, and I started to write and answer the questions I asked myself. I started to research and seek out other people who were feeling like me. That made me realize I wasn't alone in this. Other people go through this too, and other people have survived it. I read about how some are so grateful they didn't take their lives. I read about all the things they accomplished through time and healing. I still felt depressed, but there was a spark of inspiration and a little light of hope in me.

I started to research natural things that would help me get into better moods. I watched YouTube videos and listened to mental health advisers. As my research deepened, I discovered so many things about depression and suicide and how it is also a spiritual battle. I never knew that suicide and depression were a spiritual battle as well as a mental one. That caused me to dig even deeper into the Bible.

I researched about what God had to say about depression and suicide, what negative spiritual things are happening concerning suicide and depression. My discovery was truly insightful, because I realized everything I was anxious about was just negative thoughts repeated over and over in my mind. I always felt like something was taunting me or teasing me, bringing up old things that happened, all kinds of negative comments that had been said to me over my lifetime. When I felt my lowest, it seemed like everything that ever happened or I ever did and everything that went wrong hit me all at once.

I was unaware all these negative thoughts being thrown at me were demonic attacks. I would accept the thoughts as my own. I never knew Satan had anything to do with how I was feeling. Later, I discovered these demonic attacks on your mind come against you the worst when you're exhausted, hungry, and not sleeping properly. Basically, he attacks when you have a moment of weakness, he attacks when things happen, and he attacks when you're completely overwhelmed, exhausted, and didn't have enough to eat. This is when he comes against your mind and overwhelms you with thoughts of hopelessness.

I started to keep a journal of all of the times I felt overwhelmed and depressed and hopeless, and all the thoughts and things that would come to my mind, and I started to pray:

In Jesus' name I have hope and a future. Like God's word tells me, I can do all things through Christ who strengthens me. I am not hopeless, I am hopeful. I'm not afraid but faithful, and my life will have purpose and meaning. I will do all the things that God allows me to do. I will finish my life and see it through to the end, and no evil force can stop me. Amen.

As the days went on, I got a little bit stronger. I started to build strength mentally. When negative thoughts came against me, I knew exactly where it was coming from and what it was. I knew exactly what to do. As I have gotten older, my values have changed, my priorities have changed, and I look at life in a different way.

I wish I knew at ten that people can say cruel, mean, and evil things, but those words don't define you. Most of the time, when people are bullying you and picking and teasing you, it's because they see greatness in you. You're different, you stand out, and you're unique.

I wish I would have known at thirteen that having a boyfriend should not have been my ultimate goal. A relationship so young isn't everything. Being liked or being popular or being pretty to boys isn't everything. I needed to take my time and discover what I wanted to be, and not worry so much about what people thought or try to be an adult before my time.

At fifteen, I wish I would have known that just because a guy tells you you're beautiful and you can trust him, that doesn't mean you can. Don't lie to your parents, because the rules that they set in place for you are to protect you and help you.

I wish I'd known at twenty that I didn't have to have it all figured out. I was a new adult and things would gradually come to me in time. I didn't need to have everything together or have my adult success right away.

At twenty-five, I wish I would have known that my age wasn't going to hold me back from my dreams, and in God's perfect timing things will go the way they should. Patience is everything.

I wish I knew at thirty that I didn't have to be married and I didn't have to have everything figured out. I would have avoided being with someone who wasn't for me. Time is in God's hands and I don't have to keep up with other people or what society says. I needed to trust God's perfect timing instead of trying to force things to happen before their time. Don't give up! You have purpose. You got this.

WE ARE MORE THAN OUR PAIN

Someone asked me one day, "Who are you to tell anyone anything you're not qualified for?" Some may ask and question who I am to give advice about depression. Who am I to give advice about suicide ? Look at you, look at where you worked, look at your background, look at where you come from: who are you to help anyone? Who am I to even dare to write a book about such a subject? All I have is a business degree, a few mental health certifications, and life experience. It broke my heart that a few people tried to belittle my efforts to create a program to prevent suicide in youth.

I understand to a certain extent why I'm being given a hard time, but then again it's still confusing. With the negative things happening in the world, why try to discourage my efforts to help? Why assume the worst of my intentions? It just made me realize that no matter what I do, it's always going to be someone who doesn't like me or doesn't want to acknowledge anything positive about me. It hurts, but I've realized this is the devil's way of trying to keep me from telling my story and bringing light to dark places.

All I have is a business degree, and I do amateur modeling. Who am I to try to inspire anyone, with such a questionable background? The best way I can answer that is by God's amazing grace. I am nothing in myself.

I am ordinary, but the Lord is extraordinary. I am qualified in my experience and victory over suicide. I am one who has suffered through these things and knows first-hand how devastating it can be. I can relate to all of the symptoms. I can tell you the highs and the lows. I've been there, and who better to advise? Who is more qualified than someone who is experienced in the condition and has overcome it?

If my words bless one soul, heal one hurt, inspire or uplift one child, I've accomplished something amazing. I have a long road ahead of me. I am not finished, because I believe on the other side of my problems something better is in store, something more, because the Lord is creating it.

To all the bullies, all the naysayers, all the psycho religious, all the haters, judgmental hypocrites, all the people laughing, all the ones who mistreated me and mistreat people in general, and all the self-righteous bigots, I say to them: We are still here and we are still standing. You tried to break us, you tried to stop us, but no more. I may not be where I need to be, but I'm not where I used to be, and every day I get better. Every day I get stronger and every moment there is a new possibility awaiting me.

You have to get to the point where no amount of ridicule, no amount of shame, no amount of pressure, no amount of emptiness can keep you from getting up and striving.

Sometimes when you're young, and even when you're older, things happen. It seems like the end of the world, like nothing can ever be better again. This awful thing has happened and it's crushing you from the inside out. Your heart is throbbing through your chest, your eyes are swelling up with tears and you can't hold them back. You're mentally overwhelmed. You grieve in a way that exhausts you, and the hopelessness makes you feel like joy could never be yours again, but that's a lie. It is all a lie.

Hopelessness is a lie from our ultimate enemy, the devil, and his demonic puppets that torment your mind and mentally try to rob you of joy and of peace.

They beat you up from the inside out with accusations, faults, shortcomings and failures, telling you you're never going to be good enough. Telling you you're not enough, you're worthless, bringing up old issues and old mistakes, overwhelming you to the point of no return. They nag you to just let it all go, to give up, give in to the feelings of negativity or suicide. The truth is, the devil is scared of what you will become.

He wanted me to kill myself at eighteen years old. If I had done that, I would have missed out on all the wonderful things God has allowed me to experience. Suicide would have kept me from writing my story and helping so many people out of dark places and pain. The enemy was afraid of my light and my impact. You have that same purpose and impact. He doesn't want you to ever reach your full potential because he knows it will save lives and give people hope.

Today's society doesn't want to talk about evil in this world. Many people don't even believe in God or believe the devil is real. It's a touchy subject for a lot of people. It's a lie that is destroying lives. There are many representations of Christianity in the world today. A lot of people claim to be Christians and are not, and have left a bad taste in the mouths of many people who have tried to convert to Christianity.

Please realize, these people are not God, and what they have to say out of meanness, out of carelessness, out of just being human, is not a reflection of God Himself. I say this because I have been to many churches and met people and trusted people who claimed to be Christians, but I was very disappointed to find they were imperfect humans like me. I held Christians on a pedestal of perfection.

The difference with some of them is their sin isn't visible, so they condemn you for not hiding the sin, instead of helping you heal, repent, and recover from it. In my encounters with different people, I realized no one is perfect, not even Christians, but that should not stop you from seeking the truth for yourself.

All I can say is that Jesus is my peace. He is my strength. I am a believer and I have seen Him work miracles in my life through all the chaos, through all the problems, through all the stress. It is through His strength, love, and guidance that I can even write these words today.

In the midst of my own pain and problems and adversity, I needed to take time out from my own suffering to possibly help others who are suffering with things I know too well about: depression, suicide, loneliness, despair, and grief. I don't understand everything God is doing in my life. It doesn't make any sense to me how the events in my life even work together, why certain things had to happen, or why certain things were allowed to happen. Yet every one of those events have led me up to this day.

I am still here and I'm still standing. I am a survivor, and I want other survivors to stand with me. Let's see this thing called life through to the end. Death is inevitable, so don't speed up the process by giving up and not receiving the free gift of God's love that can heal the hardest hearts and the deepest wounds.

See how it works out. Give it time. Don't get upset about getting older, or not being old enough. Don't be upset about being poor, see what you can do with what you have. Take Jesus' hand and go the distance. Walk with Him. You've tried everything else.

What do you have to lose? No other religion, no other thing on earth can give you happiness in the midst of pain.

My life is not problem-free. I still struggle. I still have financial problems. I still have ordinary everyday problems, things I'm still trying to wrap my head around to get done for myself and my daughter, but I have faith that everything will work out somehow.

No, I don't know exactly how, and I don't know when, but I know it will. I am revealing myself to you because it is selfish not to. The Lord has blessed me with a gift and I have to share it. I can't wait until everything is perfect in my life, and pretend I never had a past or wait until I have the business of my dreams or until I have a better job.

I have to tell my story now. I have to share the peace and joy I have now in my current condition. It's real, it's authentic, it's me. The world has enough artificial, counterfeit, made up fairy tales,, and shimmering, shining, materialistic-based things.

We need something real, and the people who are hurting the most need to know in the midst of their pain there is a supply of love. The emptiness in their hearts and souls can be filled. You are not hopeless, your life's not over, and there can be resolution for you. Most people want to tell you about their depression struggles once they get to this ultimate level. Nothing in life is fixed overnight.

You may wake up to the same dead-end job, struggle with forgiveness . Maybe you lost a loved one, or had a bad breakup. Something's wrong, something's causing you to feel like it's hopeless, to the point of no repair and no return, and you'd rather just be gone than to take it any longer. People need to know how to manage this kind of hopelessness in the midst of what's wrong in their lives, not after everything's better. It's all a process!

We don't have that kind of time. I know I didn't. My life is still a struggle, but I know God is working everything out for my good. A hopeless case is not hopeless unless you believe it's hopeless. Go-Go dancers or strippers, people who dance or work in those kinds of industries are looked at as hopeless cases, just society's trash. They throw you into the category of prostitutes and drug addicts. The sad truth is that so many of these women are, and they have gotten stuck in their pain. Many women get into that kind of job or profession for so many different reasons. Everyone is different, no two girls are alike, no one is the same. One could be a college student who's trying to finish school, who didn't get a scholarship or an inheritance, or her parents couldn't afford to help her get to college. She wants to have an education and she decides to help pay for that education with money from dancing.

Someone else may be a single parent. Someone else may have a drug addiction or alcohol problems, or they are numb and hurting from sexual abuse or assault. I have talked to so many women in the gentlemens clubs. A lot of them are truly sweethearts and they're just trying to get by. Many of them didn't even see themselves having to work in these kinds of places, but bills, responsibilities and habits got the best of them. That's basically what happened to me.

It's kind of depressing for a lot of women, because they feel like they don't have many options. People don't understand how you could have allowed yourself to get in this situation and a strip club or a go-go bar. They look down on you, they judge you, they write you off as no good.

The reputation of these kinds of places causes everyone to have a negative point of view, because most of the time it is true. It's a negative atmosphere full of lust, sexual desire, greed and sin. I don't justify any of the negative things that a strip club or go-go bar represents or stands for. Some people may say Christians shouldn't be affected by these types of environments, but aren't these places where light needs to be presented? Aren't those kinds of places where hurting people are going? The men go there because they are lonely, stressed or trying to have a good time, so they drink alcohol, looking for sex. The women work there for the money, habits, or financial problems overall. They're lost and need spiritual help.

The gospel needs to be spread in these places so healing can take place. Every day, my walk with the Lord has opened up my heart and mind to where I need to be, where I should be. Nothing happens overnight. Everybody's walk with the Lord is different. Everyone's faith is not going to look the same. I don't recommend or justify where I worked in my humble beginnings of understanding the gospel, but I do recognize that I'm progressing and everyone's life is different. People will forget that when you're a new Christian, all your sin and problems don't magically disappear overnight. Your salvation is not in what you have done, but what Jesus did on the cross for our sins. No, this doesn't mean you just pridefully sin and arrogantly say, "Well, God will forgive me, I can do whatever I want."

What I have realized is that when you sincerely and humbly go to God, and you recognize you're lost and your life is a mess, full of sin, full of pride, you say, "Lord, I need You and I don't want to live life my way, but Your way is better. Give me the strength to do what is right. I can't let these sins go on my own. I need help."

The Lord will start doing work on the inside of your heart and mind. You will naturally start to transition away from old habits. Jesus will gradually help you put down habits you no longer want in your life. That's the Holy Spirit working on you and guiding you. The Lord knows when we honestly are tired and we are serious about a relationship with Him.

It will be a struggle and a process, but the freedom in your mind and body will be so worth it. The peace I have now is incredible. It's priceless. I don't feel like I'm missing out not doing what everyone else is doing. All the parties, drugs, drinking, sex, and selfish lifestyles. None of that can compare to the peace I have in Jesus. It's rewarding to say no to things that once had a hold on me. Sometimes you may fall down, back into old habits, but Jesus won't leave you there. He will keep helping you get back on track. He has patience with you and forgiveness for you that the world doesn't.

There will come a time in my life that everything I've been through will be an awesome testimony. Fight the good fight of faith, many things have happened to me in my life. A lot is still going on and I'm not giving up. I have made a conscious decision to keep fighting the good fight of faith. I'll have a better job where I can be a blessing to people who can relate to things I've been through and things I continue to go through.

If your state of mind isn't positive in your current circumstances and you don't have peace, the truth is the major changes happen on the inside of your heart and soul, then the physical changes will happen. You can have peace and joy right where you're at because you trust where God is taking you.

Have faith and positive thoughts about your circumstances right now. In that dead-end job right now. In the sickness of a family member or an illness you may be dealing with yourself. The loss of a loved one and addiction to drugs. If you can't have optimism right in the middle of your problem, you won't be able to see past it to have a positive future.

This is what Jesus does. He makes everything new. He gives you the ability to be happy, joyous, peaceful uplifted and inspired right where you are. He empowers you to change your life and lead you in a new direction. As your faith builds, so does your life, because as a person thinks, a person will become. If you believe negatively about yourself and your future, how will things get better? They can't. We need the hope God gives to get us through life.

This is a bit more than positive thinking. Faith is taking God at His word and trusting in Jesus to get you over the hurdle and through obstacles and across the mountains in your life.

It's much more than positive thinking. Jesus builds you up. Jesus gives you these positive thoughts. Jesus gives you inspiration. Jesus fills you up with love and understanding and surpasses your human condition. He gives you something that is beyond this world.

The world says you're not good enough. The world says you can't make it, or you are in the way, but God created you to be here. If the people of the world who see themselves as superior had the ultimate power over your life, certain people who look like you wouldn't even exist.

If they could genetically modify human beings based on intellect, race and skill sets, so many people would be left out. The fact remains: you were made and designed on purpose. You have a divine destiny. I'm realizing that, and even writing this I'm stepping into mine. You have a future right now, even in the midst of your problems. There is something amazing for you, but you have to believe it, be patient, have faith and see your life through to the end to find it.. I feel so full of hope. I'm in expectation of miracles and I truly believe there is a special blessing coming to everyone reading these words.

DEPRESSIONS TERROR

The Terror of Gloom. I have depression. I feel all alone. Everything pulls at my heart, my emotions, my thoughts. Other people's words or lack of attention. It doesn't really matter if things are going okay. I'm in eternal sadness, paralyzed mentally. Fighting through the tears and anxiety, the frustration and the hurt. Trying to make myself get up and do my daily chores and activities. I notice days when I don't get enough sleep. This weighs heavy on me.

Depression steps in and takes over my life. I'm reminded of every failure, every mean word, every disappointment, every heartache, heartbreak and every problem. My heart and my head are overwhelmed with thoughts. I'm imprisoned. I'm stuck, yet I'm free. I can't seem to get out of this cage I created mentally. I'm exhausted: exhausted with life, exhausted with myself. Exhausted with trying to be strong. Sometimes I just need a break. A break from life. This is what it must feel like to be at the edge of reason. Suicidal thoughts.

Needing that rest, a break from it all. Feeling as though death would be a source of relief. This heavy burden on my mind and my heart is too much to bear. I'm broken-hearted, I'm split in two. My love runs dry and my wounds drip blue. I feel like I've been run over and life has dragged me down. I'm in the pit so deep, deep underground, yet I'm above in my room. In this hollow space between time and my mind, there is no escape. What is this dragging, this longing for this desperation that I feel? Why am I overwhelmed in grief? Why is my heart so ill?

What is this that is taking me under? Making me feel like death would be a slumber. Why is my sky gray? Yet when I look out the window, I see the sun. Take this death that I live from me. It is agonizing. It is dreadful. It is a pain. How horrible it must be to feel this kind of pain, this kind of hurt. It has no name.

Your tears drip on a windowpane. With every drop it sounds the same. Is this what happens to your victim, as death seeps in to engulf them in grief and swallow them in pain. How dare you come into my house? How dare you hang over me, steal my peace, my joy, and my sanity? Who are you, this thing, this dark gloom, this robber, this thief, this doom.

This was a poem I wrote in my most hurting moment. If you understand this kind of pain and frustration, pray with me right now.

Father God, take all depression and suicide from me. Heal my broken heart. Heal my hurts and pains. Help me recover and allow me to be blessed with peace and comfort in Jesus' name. Amen.

The pain and suffering can be very overwhelming. It's hard to see any hope when so much is going wrong, but there is hope.

WHAT ARE YOU GRATEFUL FOR?

When life is constantly spinning you in multiple directions and you feel lost, confused and full of anxiety, this is the perfect time to take a moment and reflect on what is right in your life! Consider the things you do have control over and all the many things you have to be grateful for.

Counting your blessings on a regular basis keeps your mind from drifting into dark areas. It's easy to forget what's going right when we focus all our attention to what's going wrong. Sometimes we get so caught up with trying to do everything and trying to take on more responsibility than we can handle, we lose sight of the things right in front of us.

I remember when I had a savings goal of $3,000. I had four jobs: working in a beauty supply store, driving for Uber, professional make-up artist, and even waiting tables at a restaurant. I overwhelmed myself trying to get to my goal. I wasn't sleeping properly or eating right, and I was mentally exhausted.

I found out later when you push your body and mind past their capacity, they start to not function properly. Sleep deprivation and exhaustion, alongside unhealthy eating habits, can throw your entire system out of whack. I was so depressed and overwhelmed with everything, feeling like a failure, because I couldn't do everything I wanted in the unrealistic time frame I set for myself.

I focused so much on getting the money saved and being ahead, I forgot to live and take care of myself. I didn't take time to rest. I didn't take a day off for myself to relax and sleep well. I didn't eat right or drink enough water. I pushed myself too far. Without realizing, I was compromising my health, not only my physical health, but my mental health as well.

At this point in my life, I had to realize if I don't have my health or my life, the money will be worthless. Your health and overall well-being are your wealth, and if you create a healthy balance between work and rest, your goals will be met. Ask yourself: *If the risk outweighs the reward, is it really a reward? Is it worth the risk? What else can I do to create balance?*

What am I thankful for? Is this lifestyle really what I want long-term? Do I really need to work this hard? Do I take out time for myself to be at peace? What can I do to protect my inner peace? I realized that if obtaining my goals meant putting my life at risk and gambling with the outcome, it's probably best I reconsider my approach. Life is too short.

When we become consumed by pride or greed, we can lose touch with what's most important. When you trust God to provide for your needs, you gain understanding about the true purpose of your life. You will quickly see it's not about trying to get all the money or accomplishments or being rich and famous. Life isn't about being popular, being liked by everyone else or having the world's approval.

Without God at the center of your life, you will live in a way that will leave you feeling lonely, worthless, scared, depressed, lost, confused, anxious, overwhelmed, and just hopeless. The world is a scary place, and so many of us try to be tough and roll with the punches of life, because we believe this is how things are, a rat race to get to the finish line by any means necessary. Trying to outdo the next person or feel accomplished and worthy, based on material gain. The sad thing is we only come to realize this truth after many mistakes. Having more money doesn't always alleviate the problems or make you happy. Having what we want doesn't fulfill us on a deeper level. People try to fill this empty void in their lives with friends or relationships, money, drugs, sex, popularity, partying and anything that we use to determine our individual worth. There's an emptiness on the inside of your heart that money can't fill, sex can't fill, shopping and friends can't fill, cars and material possessions can't fill, drugs and alcohol can't fill.

None of the accomplishments you can ever have will fill that empty void in your heart. We as human beings are on this quest to feel complete, to feel acceptance, to be accomplished, and have value. What we fail to realize is our completeness is in God through Christ Jesus. When I was young, I rolled my eyes at the idea that everything I needed to feel whole and complete in my own skin was in Jesus. That sounded a little out there to me, but after running into hard life lessons, I fell to my defeat by trying things my way. I gave Jesus a chance and I honestly get it now.

I was so stubborn, wanting my own way. I refused to go to God until I had no other option. We have to be careful pushing against the grain of life, trying to get ahead by doing things our way, and not seeking wisdom. Life has a way of throwing curve balls that can make you feel like all your efforts are pointless. At these times I finally realized that my way of thinking and operating isn't best.

I needed help. I needed divine intervention!. So I went to God and I prayed to the Lord to help me do things the right way so I can get results without the burden of setbacks. I asked God: "Who am I? What's my purpose in life? Help me not be prideful or stubborn, to stay in bad habits that hinder me.

Lord, help me to have the grace to do Your plan and have the desires of my heart."

I prayed these prayers, and not long after things in my life turned around. I felt less pressured and anxious about everything. I didn't feel like I needed all the answers about my life. I had peace about who I was as a person, and things started to make sense. The Lord had humbled me to see things from a spiritual eye view instead of a worldly eye view. The world's opinion of me was everything on the surface, but the spiritual eye view was everything in my heart, in my soul. My true authentic self, not the person I tried to portray to the world. Someone who seemingly has it all together, but the person inside that just wanted everything to be okay and to see the good in others.

So my best advice is: Don't look at your life through the lens of the world, from social media, or through your friends or even negative opinions of yourself. Look at yourself as God sees you. That starts by having a relationship with the Lord. And it's a continuous process. Walking by faith is always seeking Jesus. This is the secret to peace. The Lord will grace you to have peace when you stay in communication with Him. I want you to ask yourself who you really are. What kind of person do you want to be? What are you grateful for? If you feel lost or empty or just confused, say this simple prayer:

Lord, fill up my heart to help me have a relationship with You through reading Your word and prayers. Help me discover my purpose that You created me for. Help me to understand your ways so I can rely on you when things in life become difficult. In Jesus' name. Amen.

I know all of your emotions are confusing and tiring at times, but remember: you aren't alone in how you feel. Many of us have been there, and it's difficult for everyone. Take the hand of the Lord and the people He has placed in your life as a positive inspiration. Everything will be okay. Believe this. You're not alone.

NECESSARY OBSTACLES

I've realized in life we come up against so many struggles and difficult seasons. What we fail to understand is that sometimes the pain in life has a deeper purpose. A bigger purpose than what we even realize. It's hard to understand because life is full of the unknown and we can't see the full picture to see where this is leading us.

I know from experience how life can be so unfair. We lose loved ones, we get broken hearts, we fail, we make mistakes, we are lonely, we feel overwhelmed. One thing all of us have in common is that we will experience some kind of tragedy in our lifetimes, unfortunately. It's a sad fact of life that something will happen, something will go wrong, and we never know when it's coming.

I've overcome many obstacles throughout my childhood, teen years, and young adult life. I've realized all the problems had something to offer me, but I couldn't see that until I made it through the storm I was facing. We are being polished and refined through these experiences. Every negative event I have experienced has given me a strength I didn't have before. The negative obstacles caused me to reflect on myself, causing me to recognize things about myself I never knew.

I've had things happen to me that I thought I'd never recover from, heartbreaks I never thought I could get over. I am the oldest of six kids from my mothers side. I have three brothers and two sisters. On my fathers side, I have two sisters and one brother. Losing my two younger brothers on my mothers side to murder made me feel like I lost a part of myself, like I was dying inside. When you're going through loss, it can seem like you'll always be in that moment of grieving and suffering. In my times of reflection after so many things have happened in my life, I realized I had a choice to make: to let these things defeat me, keep me discouraged, or to let what has happened grow me into a stronger, more adaptable person.

What really caused me to change my perspective and choose to become stronger from my experiences was the fact that so many people depended on me. My goal to inspire hope gave me a sense of purpose. We don't realize how many lives we affect, how many people we interact with, and how many people may be counting on us for inspiration or for encouragement.

At different points in my life, I definitely wanted to be selfish and not care about anyone else's feelings and what anyone else thought, because I was hurting and what I was feeling was the most important thing. But the misery I was causing myself only allowed the suffering to make my heart hard and cold. It only hurt me, and it hurt the people around me. So I decided I wasn't going to shut down or hide or run.

It's necessary to grieve. It's necessary to be in the moment of despair or hurt, to cry and just have that moment to yourself. There's no getting away from the hurt and the pain, especially when something has just happened in your life. But there is sunshine after the rain. It is possible to heal and get better.

The pain will pass. You can have peace over the problems. The choice is always up to you to live life miserably, stuck in the past, stuck in your emotions, stuck in fear or self-hate, or blaming and complaining, or you can make something positive out of the negative experience. Allow the lessons to be learned. Be a shoulder to lean on for someone else's pain and loss. Be hope to someone who feels hopeless, like you once did.

My choice to change my attitude helped me to change my perspective and helped me to be happy again. Reality is this: Our lives are not just about us. One of our biggest purposes as human beings is to help each other. Sometimes our growth comes through pain and struggle. It builds our character. It heightens our sensitivity and it humbles us.

It's unfair how life can throw all of these negative events into our lives and we have to pick up the pieces somehow and move on. Many of us have never picked up the pieces or moved on. We have shoved many issues down into our hearts or the back of our minds, trying to forget about them.

All the suffering, hurt and pain will resurface, and will affect your relationships, affect your job, affect your happiness and your productivity. We can't ignore what has happened to us and hope it just goes away. We can't stay angry, hurt and bitter, hoping it will go away somehow. Many of us are depressed from events we have almost forgotten, or things we want to forget that affect us in some way or another.

Emotional trauma can be more painful than physical trauma at times, because physical trauma heals, but emotional trauma, if not dealt with properly, only grows the wounds bigger, spilling over into areas of our lives where we are usually happy. This is the reason for moments of depression and then moments of happiness. Pain that had never been handled returns to the surface. We find ourselves struggling with issues that are unsolved, and this leaves us stuck.

Mental barriers are created from heart issues that have never been dealt with. The problem and the pain never leave us, no matter how much we laugh and smile. No matter how much we push through our lives, trying to forget. No matter how many good moments we have after that painful event. If we don't deal with the issues that have hurt us, the residue will always resurface.

There are so many people who don't talk about their problems or how they feel. They bottle up all their emotions and attempt to ignore the pain, walking through life, pretending everything is fine. This doesn't solve anything. It only leaves you susceptible to more heartache and more hurt, because you never properly dealt with the pain from your past. We have to make a decision when negative things happen to us. The decision is: "I choose to heal from this. I choose to not allow this situation to defeat (me) and take over the rest of my life. I will not run from how I feel or try to find a temporary escape. I will face problems as they come."

When you make that decision, talk to people in your life you trust. If you don't have someone you can trust, talk to a therapist. Talk to someone who can give you sound, reasonable feedback. Making this kind of decision when you're suffering makes all the difference for your situation and for your future.

Bottling up everything that happens and every pain you experience never solves anything, it only creates more heartbreak. When something else negative happens in your life, even a small issue may be blown out of proportion and will seem to be unbearable to live with because of all the unresolved issues.

You can't even begin to deal with the new issues if you have left the old problems unresolved. It's okay to vent. It's okay to get stuff off your chest. It's okay to not be okay. Don't ever let someone make you feel like your problems aren't important or not a big deal. We all process things differently, and what may not be a big deal to them may be a huge deal to you.

Only talk to people who have positive feedback and nurturing feedback to give you, because someone who doesn't care about how you feel will only make you feel worse. Pain and suffering can either build you up in the long run or tear you down. We will all experience some kind of pain and struggle in this lifetime, but what we do to heal from it makes all the difference. It is possible to heal. It is possible to have peace. It is possible to get better.

You don't have to sit in silence with anything that you're suffering with or going through. If it's important to you, it's important enough to talk about and get resolution. Don't let issues eat away at you until there's nothing left. The best part of healing from the struggles and suffering is being able to reach back and give someone else hope. Someone needs to hear your story. Someone needs what you have to offer. Your life matters and you have purpose. Believe that!

REJECTION

Growing up, I always felt like I didn't measure up to other people. I always felt like I wasn't pretty enough. I wasn't tall enough. My hair wasn't good enough. My smile wasn't good enough. I wasn't smart enough. I wasn't where a lot of other people were. I constantly compare myself to other people. That always made me feel as if I could never be more than what I was.

I didn't learn until I was much older that who I am and my self-worth are not measured by the world. It's not measured by how other people treat me or if I get compliments or I'm told I did a good job, or even if my family tells me they're proud of me. My significance could not ever be measured by other people's point of view, because no matter how many people told me I was beautiful, no matter how much my mom and my family and my grandmother would tell me I was smart and they were proud of me, I did not see value in myself because I felt as if I didn't measure up. I wasn't as pretty as other girls, or I wasn't as slim as some of my classmates or I didn't get the grades in certain subjects. So I measured myself based on my physical appearance, my social status, my popularity, and other people's opinion of me. If anyone didn't approve of me, I felt as if I wasn't enough. I felt like I didn't deserve love. I didn't deserve my dreams or my goals or a good job or good relationships or friends.

Some people with low self-esteem and a poor self-image tend to become people pleasers. They settle for jobs, they settle all throughout life, they settle in their love relationships, they settle with their friendships. And when they're not being treated well, they feel like this is the best they can do and they don't really deserve to have someone treat them with the utmost respect, because they feel they're not worthy of it.

The world today puts an emphasis on perfection, flawless beauty and materialistic values as the American dream, in a sense. If you do not have the looks, the money, the popularity, the smarts, the background, the right skin color, the right abilities and talents, the world convinces you that you're nothing, less than.

The world's eye view is very shallow, very corrupt, and very vain. There is nothing wrong with being beautiful. There is nothing wrong with having money or popularity. There is nothing wrong with wanting to be successful and wanting to have materialistic gain, but the problem arises when all of our self-worth and values are based on these things.

The world we live in leaves out so many people who are less fortunate, who don't have the social status, the money, the looks, the athletic abilities and talents or even intelligence. The world looks down on those who don't fit certain criteria. The way of the world rejects and leaves out so many people.

It makes you wonder: With all these people on the earth, are some just worthless? Are some just mistakes? Some have seemingly won the genetic lottery, equipped with everything, while others of us have very little.

Are we just existing by chance or luck? If we don't measure up to the world's view and standards, is our life meaningless? The answer is **No**! You are more than what you realize.

The world's point of view limits the truth about your unique existence. It's a natural feeling to want to fit in. It's a natural feeling to want to be liked and want to be successful. To want to have things other people may have.

What I realized in my own journey is that I had to discover who I am as an individual, and what my unique responsibility is here on the earth, without trying to mimic what the world is trying to make me conform into, only to be a copycat and failing miserably. I had to realize I can never be good at being someone else. I can only be good at being who I am. Who I'm supposed to be.

So I started to do some research, studying, and praying, really looking within my own heart, within my own mind, and within my own spirit. Discovering who I am. What makes me unique? What are my talents and abilities? In what areas and subjects am I very intelligent? What excites me? What moves me? What motivates me? What gets me so happy or thrilled? And also, what makes me sad? What makes me angry? What makes me question everything? I took time with myself to zone out the world, zone out social media, zone out even the pressures of family and friends, zone out unrealistic expectations, hurts and pains, and really looked within to see who I really was and what made me unique and different.

The confusing thing about growing up and not knowing exactly where you fit in is that it can cause you to lose yourself, because you're so busy trying to fit into a mold that society, family, friends and other people expect. Sometimes we put pressure on ourselves to try to make ourselves fit into a mold that really isn't for us. A place meant for someone else. I've had to take the time to realize even though I admired a certain ability and talent in another person, I had to just be happy I could witness them in their element, instead of trying to have it for myself.

I tried to play the guitar. I tried to play the violin. I tried to do all these things that were amazing and was exciting for me, but the curiosity of these things only lasted a moment. I wasn't truly passionate enough about playing the guitar or the violin to actually execute it to fulfillment.

Just because it would be really cool to be able to play the guitar or the violin or the piano or other appealing things, I had to realize those things didn't appeal enough for me to accomplish what was needed to master the ability. These things were outside of my purpose and it was outside of my passion. I discovered I needed to have passion to bring my goals to life.

Your purpose is tied into your passion. I needed to be very passionate about anything that I wanted to accomplish in my life. Just wanting to do it or seeing someone else have certain things was not enough.

I began to realize my self-esteem is not caught up in being what the world wants me to be. I have a choice. I have an option, and I do not have to accept mediocrity, poverty or feeling as if I'm not good enough. I can be beautiful in my own right, and I can live my life to the fullest even if I'm not a millionaire, the world's next top model, or an actor, or drive an expensive car, or have all the shoes and clothes, or a large social media following or all the approval.

I can be inspired and hopeful even if I don't have it all. My self-worth changed as I started to realize how the Lord viewed me. It took the pressure off my life to copy and measure up to the world's view of beauty. Self-esteem is typically defined as confidence in one's own worth or abilities.

As a Christian, I define self-esteem as having confidence that I am who God says I am.

It's not dependent on my own abilities (those can be so unreliable!), but instead on knowing God will equip me for the work He has set out for me to do.

Psalm 139:13–14
For you created my inmost being;
you knit me together in my mother's womb.
I praise you because I am fearfully and wonderfully made;
your works are wonderful,
I know that full well.

I love this verse. When everything about me feels wrong and broken and misfit in this world, I can rely on the fact that God created me just the way I am on purpose. You weren't a mistake. You were fearfully and wonderfully made by Almighty God, who does everything on purpose. That right there is enough reason to walk with your head held high!

Truly it has changed my life to look at my possibilities through how God sees me and how God views me as a person. It took so much of the pressure of being more and doing more all the time off my back. I have a very humble perspective and it's beautiful.

The Lord has opened up doors and opportunities to me that I never would have dreamed of. 2019 was the most surprising and rewarding time in my life. It was like all my prayers were being answered at this appointed time. I started the suicide prevention program, because I felt a strong passion to not only help my daughter but to help other people, too. I researched and found that suicide rates were extremely high all around the world. I felt like I could help in some small way. So I took a leap of faith and started reaching out to Lifeline National Suicide Prevention and TeenLine. I called up many businesses to ask if they would be interested in allowing me to host events to raise funds to help teens and young adults with depression and suicide. To my surprise, many restaurants and major department stores like Target were so happy to help me accomplish my goal. I was able to help so many young people in my local area.

Not long after starting the Project Your Life Matters Program, my modeling started to take off. I was invited to model in London, Las Vegas, LA, Hawaii and Paris, France. I even was blessed with my dream vehicle, a lime green Jeep Wrangler. It was such an overwhelming time of joy in my life. I was in complete shock and amazement at everything that was happening.

I remember just breaking down in tears of joy, because God had blown my mind. In His faithfulness, His love, and His promises, He allowed me to experience things I prayed about as a little girl, dreams I thought were out of my reach. Jesus showed me that if I wait on Him, He would make my dreams come true. I thought I was too old to keep pursuing a modeling career, but God showed me that time is in His hands. At thirty-five years old, God has blessed me to appear years younger than my actual age. My daughter looks more like a twin sister, which is so unique. Jesus renewed my youth, so my age wasn't even a factor with my modeling career. God showed up for me and showed out in such an amazing way, all throughout my life.

Beyond the trips I experienced, and material things, the most precious gift God has given me is my daughter. I remember when she was three years old. She saw me crying about something that happened. She said, "It's okay, Mommy, don't cry, I love you."

God has turned everything that was meant to destroy me into something beautiful. God's love and peace surround me, and I know all is well.

Life is still a struggle, no matter what you have. We must realize there will always be something going on, we will never be free of problems, trials and tribulations. But we can be at peace and we can have understanding that will release us from stress and anxiety. We as human beings feel the need to have complete and utmost control, and our lack of control causes us to panic, to be stressed out and full of anxiety.

At times, we don't know how we're going to pay our bills. We don't know how the promotion or job outcome will be. We don't know what the diagnosis will be. What is coming around the corner next. If relationships will work. If we'll be betrayed. Our lives seem to always be slipping through our fingers and we never can hold on to much of anything. It's overwhelming and stressful that life has no guarantees.

It seems so pointless to even try, but the hope God gives allows understanding through His word. Getting to know Him, knowing the purpose of life, knowing why all the evil is in the world, knowing why He has appointed a certain time for all of this negativity to be done away with. We don't have to be perfect to come to Him, to pray to Him, or to ask for things we need. We are riddled with guilt, with pressure, with so many responsibilities and so many hurts and pains we have tried to bury at the bottom of our hearts, in hope that one day all of it will just go away.

Unfortunately, it won't, and that beats up on our self-confidence. We feel so helpless and out of control, but I say this: if we will allow the Lord in our lives and start looking at life through God's perspective, our whole entire world will change. One thing about God is that He accepts us as we are and where we are in life right now.

The world may not accept you, and that's okay. I am the world's reject, but I am God's elect, and because He has allowed me to be who I am and allowed me to know that I am chosen by Him, that gives me hope, inspiration and joy. Once my perspective changed about myself, knowing I have a place in the world in my own unique way, I was more inspired to do what was in my heart to do. I help people and live my life hopeful.

Here is a simple prayer if you have not yet given your life to Jesus and invited Him into it:

Jesus, I believe You are the Son of God, that You died on the cross to rescue me from sin and death and to restore me to the Father. I choose now to turn from my sins, my self-centeredness, and every part of my life that does not please You. I choose You. I give myself to You. I receive Your forgiveness and ask You to take Your rightful place in my life as my Savior and Lord. Come reign in my heart, fill me with Your love and Your life, and help me to become a person who is truly loving—a person like You. Restore me, Jesus. Live in me. Love through me. Thank You, God. In Jesus' name I pray. Amen.

Your life matters. You are more than you know, and you have value. Don't give up, don't give in.

PRAYERS FOR PEACE

Dear God, I come before You to lay my panic and anxiety at Your feet. When I'm crushed by my fears and worries, remind me of Your power and Your grace. Fill me with Your peace as I trust in You, and You alone. I know I can't beat this on my own, but I also know that I have You, Lord, and You have already paid the ultimate price to carry my burdens

For this I thank You. Amen.

Dear Jesus,

You are the strength of my life;

You are my rock, my fortress and my protector; therefore, whom shall I be afraid?

You are my shield, my strong-tower and my stronghold.

I will call to You because You are worthy to be praised.

So, Father, I thank you for being my strength and My God in whom I trust, Amen.

— Psalm 27:1b

Heavenly Father, When I feel crushed by my own worries, lift my mind and help me to see the truth.

When fear grips me tight and I feel I cannot move, free my heart and help me to take things one step at a time.

When I can't express the turmoil inside, calm me with Your quiet words of love.

I choose to trust in You, each day, each hour, each moment of my life.

I know deep down that I am in Your grace, forgiven, restored by Your sacrifice. You have set me free. Amen.

God, who is more than we can ever comprehend, helps us to seek You, and You alone.

Help us to stand before all that we could do and seek what You would do, and do that.

Lift from us our need to achieve all we can be and instead, surrender to what You can be in us.

Give us ways to refrain from the busyness that will put us on edge and off center, give us today Your peace.

Loving God, please grant me peace of mind and calm my troubled heart. My soul is like a turbulent sea. I can't seem to find my balance, so I stumble and worry constantly.

Give me the strength and clarity of mind to find my purpose and walk the path You've laid out for me. I trust your love, God, and know that You will heal this stress. Just as the sun rises each day against the dark of night.

Please bring me clarity with the light of God. In Your name I pray. Amen.

UNBOTHERED

As a kid, I would experience bullying and everyone would tell me the same thing: Just ignore it. Don't give into what they're saying. Just let it go. So when issues came up in school, I started to not say anything. I kept it to myself because I knew what the answer would be. This is the same truth for me today as an adult. I'm still being told to ignore the haters, don't feed into their negativity, don't believe what they say. The advice is absolutely right, but is it enough?

Is it enough to simply just ignore negativity? Regardless, if you are an elementary student, a middle school student, or a high school student, or maybe you are in your twenties or maybe you're older. Maybe other issues are weighing you down and people have constantly told you to be unbothered, don't let the negativity affect you. One thing I have realized is that no one has given any more insight into how to deal with an issue other than ignore it or how to not be bothered by negativity or issues that come up in life.

So inadvertently we train ourselves to ignore our emotions, to be "unbothered." We try to let things roll off our backs. The old saying is to "roll with the punches," let it go, but does it ever really leave us? Do the issues ever really just go away? For some of us, it may be true. You can ignore negativity and you're fine. Your "unbothered" self-confidence is solid and you don't feel the need to be reassured of anything.

But for many of us this is not true. When someone diminishes your character or mistreats you, humiliates you, or when your heart is broken, you can't simply pretend everything is fine. Maybe something has happened in your life and you don't know what to do, there is no way to be unbothered. Most people's solution is to just go on about life as usual. This idea that we are weak because we have feelings and emotions is all wrong.

This idea is forced on men, women, and on our youth. Society today tells us to just keep going, no time to stop and reflect or heal. Just keep it pushing no matter what, ignore what hurts you and pretend you're fine when it does. Smile, show that happy mask for the world, but be broken behind closed doors.

You deserve happiness that isn't just a show on social media but a reality, even when no one else is looking. The world today wants us to be numb to pain and problems, even when grieving the loss of a loved one. We have to let it go and go back to work as usual. There's no time to grieve or even sleep. Hyped up on caffeine and energy drinks, we barely can function to get through the day. The world's way is to go and keep going.

The fact is, we must slow down and face what is happening and deal with our emotions. We are not robots, we are not machines. We need love, care, and positive outlets for our mental and emotional health. When you're constantly pushing everything that happens to you in the back of your mind, you will eventually explode. You're a ticking time bomb without even realizing it.

Some people start to have panic attacks, anxiety, and nervousness. Some have crying spells and don't know why. Some people get so overwhelmed with negative feelings they lose interest in going out or doing anything. Most people don't realize this is the body's way of trying to detox itself of negative emotions. Just like when we eat an unhealthy diet and come down with symptoms, and the doctor tells us we have an underlying condition, sickness is the body's response.

The truth is, changes have to be made, but if we are unaware that we need changes in our lives, our mental health suffers the consequences. We need an emotional detox from negative things in our lives to keep us healthy, mentally and physically. We have to properly deal with life's issues as they come. No matter if it's bullying, a loss in the family, a recent break-up, health issues, bad news, mistreatment, bad habits, or something that's out of our control.

We are very complex, and our connection isn't just physical, it's emotional and spiritual, mind, body, and soul. Anything out of sync can cause all kinds of issues, ultimately affecting our everyday lives. Healing and restoration are needed. Ignoring issues never solved anything.

One of the best ways to get the most out of an emotional detox is to treat yourself with kindness, compassion, and love. Forgive yourself for the things you cannot change or control and move on from your past mistakes. Accept yourself for who you are and make time each day to do things that make you truly happy.

Know your truth. Know your worth. Build your self-confidence and your esteem by realizing who you are as an individual. Positive outlets of expression always heal the soul, get positive feedback from friends and family, and can also heal wounds of the heart.

Many of the teens I've worked with have experienced bullying. I ask them to go to friends and family members and ask them to list all their good qualities. I want you to do the same thing. Ask them what they love about you and how you positively impact their lives. Take all of these positive affirmations and read them out loud to yourself. And in times when someone challenges your self-worth, remember this list and let these truths be in your thoughts always.

> Lord, help me to stay encouraged to have a positive outlook in my life. To remember my worth is not determined by other people's opinions of me but, who You have created me to be in Jesus name amen.

THE BIGGER PICTURE

What is success? Is it having everything you ever wanted? Is it having millions of dollars for your dream job? Maybe success is all of these things, but I believe it is so much more. Success to me is triumph over mental barriers and obstacles. Fame and fortune are nice. Having the newest car is great. Having plenty of money in the bank is awesome.

Don't count yourself out because you don't have all the money in the world or everything together. If you have overcome a difficult time in your life, you are a walking testimony of perseverance and strength. You are a success story and someone struggling may need your advice and courage to get through a difficult time in their lives. Many times, we measure our self-worth by the world's point of view that success is materialistic gain, qualifying you as a person of high status and accomplishment.

The world leaves out the people who have overcome drug addiction or the people who have made it through a difficult childhood or an abusive situation. They leave out the people who have lost loved ones, people who have been homeless, the depressed, people who have been suicidal and heartbroken.

Many of us have a success story of how we persevered and overcame a difficult time in our lives. A time where we had no hope.

Success is having the strength to keep going when everything falls apart. In society today, the most broken people in the world are rejected and pushed aside and counted out, but there is hope if you are willing to believe you can overcome whatever obstacle you are facing today. Your success story is your ability to persevere against all odds. **It is possible.** You can make it. You can get through this.

Break down every mental wall of negativity. Break free of your mental prison of everything that is holding you back and telling you your life is meaningless or worthless. *It's not true.* The first step to recovering from any kind of negativity in life is to believe you are worth fighting for. **Your life is worth fighting for. Your dreams are worth fighting for. Your health is worth fighting for.** *Stop accepting negativity, negative thoughts, negative people, negative situations.* You are worth more than what you have been subjected to. Tell yourself each day: "I am worth fighting for, my life matters."

YOUR LIFE HAS VALUE

It's truly sad in today's world that people are still bullying and giving out so much negative criticism. It's as if they build themselves up by tearing others down mentally and emotionally. They don't even care if they're torturing you to the point of feeling like there is no purpose to live. We live in a very selfish world where so many people have lost love, care, and concern for others, and they feel good knocking the next person down.

Well I'm here to tell you that you matter, you have a purpose, you are unique, and you are here on this earth for a reason. It doesn't matter who is against you, who doesn't like you, who doesn't like the way you look. Remind yourself: you matter, you have a purpose, and these people who have all these negative things to say about you are irrelevant to your future and irrelevant to your life. Their opinion doesn't define who you are. Even when you have negative thoughts about yourself, remind yourself you matter. You matter to your family, you matter to the people who care about you, and you matter because you have a right to be happy in your own skin.

We cannot accept every negative voice that speaks over us; we have to reject the mental negativity we bring on ourselves and outside negativity from other people. Don't be defined by what someone else thinks about you, be defined by who you are and who you are working to be. Yes, it's definitely easier said than done when you're being bombarded everyday with someone's negative opinion and point of view. Being physically mistreated, emotionally mistreated, and mentally mistreated is overwhelming, but you don't have to suffer in silence and you don't have to suffer alone.

Stand up for yourself by first saying, "I matter. I have value. I have goals, dreams and ambitions. I'm here on this earth and I matter. What I want and what I need matter." Say it until you believe it, because once you believe you truly do matter and your life has value, you won't sit back on the sidelines and allow negativity to keep dragging you into pits of despair. One of my pet peeves is people who try to get a laugh at someone else's expense. They don't care how they make that person feel or how it affects someone. It's a form of bullying and it's really unfortunate that so many people don't care about anyone else's feelings but their own. Respect should be given to everyone, but first we have to respect ourselves and not accept negative behavior that crushes our spirits and puts us down. Never suffer in silence and never, ever let anyone make you believe any mistreatment is something you deserve, because you don't.

SMALL ACCOMPLISHMENTS STILL COUNT

Take each day one day at a time. What I realized about depression is you have to take each day as it comes. Trying to plan too far out in advance can overwhelm you and keep you stuck where you're at. Taking baby steps and small strides toward your goals can get you closer to where you need to be.

Depression. Sometimes you don't even want to get in the shower. You don't even want to get out of bed. You have to force yourself to get something to eat or you overeat. It's difficult to do normal activities like, paying bills & grocery shopping. These activities seem so small, but they can be overwhelming and too much for someone suffering with depression.

Set Small Goals. The best solution to this is to set goals for yourself. Small ones at first: brush your teeth, wash your face, get in the shower and view even the small tasks as accomplishments.

Depression can keep you down and out to the point that even getting proper hygiene is something you can't push yourself to do. Create small goals and accomplish them, and as you accomplish two small goals, keep adding things to your list and moving throughout your day. As I suffered from depression, I had to give myself many pep talks. I had to motivate myself and be thankful for what I had. I had to reflect on the positive things going on in my life and deflect the things that were negative in my life.

I realized if I lay in bed and didn't pay my bills, I would have another problem on my hands. I would be evicted. If I didn't eat, I wouldn't be healthy. I wouldn't feel any better than I did right then. I would be creating more of a depressive state. So in that realization I motivated myself by saying, "I can get in the shower. I can start my day."

Get your mind off the things that are upsetting. Think back on a time when you had a lot of fun and you enjoyed yourself. Think back on positive memories or even positive ambitions or goals you may have, and let those be your focal point.

Depression will not go away on its own. If you need to talk to someone, if you need to go to the doctor, if you need help, take those first steps in the right direction of getting the help you need. Just lying in bed or sobbing or crying won't get you to the next level of being better and being healed.

So in the moments where you have time to think positive thoughts or enough thoughts outside of your feelings and your emotions, pick up the phone, make a call. Tell someone you trust what you're going through. Don't suffer in silence alone. Get help. Sometimes it's good to talk to someone who can motivate you to make the call to get to the doctors, to get the medication you need. Sometimes someone else's insight on your situation can help you see things differently. Knowing someone else cares about you can get you to a point of healing and relief, to get the help you need. You do not have to suffer in silence alone. Asking for help does not make you weak, it actually makes you strong.

BUMPS IN THE ROAD

In March 2019, I had a trip to London, to model. I've also traveled to a few other places, and I've noticed that none of my travel experiences have been perfect. I was on a flight from Charlotte, North Carolina to London. I was seated beside a man who was seven feet tall. Long story short, I was being squashed. I tried to ask the person to maybe move over to the other empty seat, but he refused, even though I asked him and he saw I was very uncomfortable. There was an empty seat available to him, so he could lean over into two seats instead of leaning over on me. I tried to get to another seat that was not occupied, but the plane was pretty full. I tried to get comfortable and relax.

Unfortunately, I couldn't, and this twelve-hour flight seemed to take an eternity. My shoulder hurt, my whole right side was in pain. I tried to ask for another seat and there wasn't anything available. I was exhausted. I was hoping I could possibly get a few hours of sleep to relax, but nope. At this moment, I realized I had a few options. I could sit there and argue. Be angry, loud, and nasty. I could just sit here in agonizing pain, or I could try to make myself comfortable and tell myself, "I'll get through this and the flight will be over before I know it."

None of these options would give me much relief, but I knew if I stayed positive this situation would pass. I definitely realized losing my cool and getting out of character might not be the best solution. So I got a pillow and wedged it between me and the other person in my row. I got myself a little comfortable the best I could, and I stayed positive. This moment in my life was very frustrating. I decided to reflect on the good instead allowing this situation to ruin my day. I had so much to be thankful for. I was on a flight to London, somewhere I had been dreaming and hoping and wishing to go for so many years. The plane was safely arriving at my destination.

In life, we have to look at the bigger picture. When we have a moment of suffering or moments of frustration, if we let the frustrations of life knock us down mentally, we won't be able to move past the negative moment. Ten years ago, I used to let things that happened destroy my day. If a certain thought came to my mind, I was stuck in the past and it controlled my life. I definitely understand how the trials of life can be so irritating and frustrating. I realized if we're not careful, we'll let these things build up in us and take away from our present, from our future, and from our possibilities. This is why having patience, discipline and self-control are key.

Have an attitude of positivity even when things go wrong, even when everything around you seems to be crumbling. To make it through the difficult time in your life requires patience to make the right decisions in the midst of your suffering. Reject negative thoughts that seem to cause you to think this situation will last forever, when the truth is it won't and it can't.

What I mean by making the right decisions in your suffering is basically not letting yourself go or letting yourself be so down or upset until your day is ruined. Don't let what goes wrong or what people say take away from your overall life.

Having an attitude of positivity is definitely easier said than done. Some situations are so outrageous, unbearable, and insane, until you can't help but get out of character, get out of sorts, feel depressed, and just not even want to care.

We have to train ourselves in these moments to start building ourselves back up so that once this moment passes, we can move on with our lives, instead of staying stuck in the past or stuck in a moment. I used to reflect on my past on a regular basis and relive disappointments and heartaches as if they were happening right now. Without realizing it, I was taking away from the possibilities of today by reflecting on the past. Of course, it's hard to forget, it's hard to let go. I've realized that even if I revisit the past, I have to remind myself I'm not there anymore, so I'm not stuck in the anger of the hurt and suffering of what was done or what had happened in those moments.

Sometimes it's necessary to revisit past events and issues. Forgetting or ignoring them doesn't work. We have to face our past and our problems head-on. Masking them or brushing them under the rug only hurts us in the long run. As we push things deeper and deeper down in our emotions, they always seem to pop back up, causing us to relive the pain and the suffering. All it does is cause a continuous process of depression and anxiety and hurt. This keeps us from healing and learning the lessons we should be able to key in on.

Over the years, I've learned to have discipline over my emotions and patience with myself. The bumps in the road that come along in life are frustrating. The truth is, there's always something trying to steal your joy. You have a choice in these moments: to stay frustrated or choose not to allow it to take over your entire day. You could be frustrated with being stuck in traffic, or maybe your employer overlooked you for promotion, a relationship ended, your flight was delayed, or you were seated with someone who made you uncomfortable.

Whatever the issue may be, we have to be able to take a step back, breathe, process everything from a positive perspective, include the bigger picture, and realize this situation will not be this way forever. There is no need for you to stay stuck in any moment that doesn't build you up. When I'm going through a very difficult time and something happens that really puts me in a bad mood or causes me to be very frustrated or angry, I dwell on the good moments I've had in my life. I take time to write in my journal about things in my life that are good, all my blessings, all my hopes, all my dreams, and things I am doing to actually make my dreams a reality.

In moments of despair and hopelessness, I refer back to my writings. I refer back to these pages, and when I see what I have written about all the good things I have to look forward to, I'm encouraged to keep working hard, to keep trying, and not give up. This applies to so many things in life, because the hardships really pull at our self-esteem, our self-worth. When we're being bombarded with obstacles and tragedies, it's like life has just hit us like a hurricane and everything is wrong.

Sometimes it's more than you can bear and can seem as though everything is off. In these moments, it's easy to get in a depressive state of hopelessness. It becomes difficult to see anything good when nothing good is happening. The truth is, even in your suffering there is something you can do to build on the good in your life: a positive attitude, creative writing, art, dancing, singing, journaling, talking to a friend. A positive outlet allows you to be in a hopeful state of mind.

We have to be creative with life. We have to look at life in a different perspective, in a different angle, to really get the best results. Sometimes it seems as if we are out of options or solutions, and nothing can be done, but if we take the time to look at life, to reflect, definitely something can be done. Don't be stubborn, don't be so prideful that we don't ask for help.

Strength is not keeping your emotions bottled up. That goes for men and women. Strength is allowing yourself time to heal. If that healing process involves you talking to your family and friends, a therapist or a doctor, that is a very strong decision, because now you will be equipped with what you need to heal and to grow.

It's challenging to keep fighting and pushing through your situation, but please realize you don't have to do it alone. Weigh your options in every area of your life, whether it's improving your health, circumstances, your job/career, your family life, relationships, finances.

We have to build somewhere. The best place to start is exactly where we are now. Put things in motion and in place to improve the situation. When I started doing this for myself, I started to see my possibilities. I gained a positive perspective and an understanding that I will have problems and things will go wrong, but I can get through them. Keep an attitude of hope and perseverance.

MAKE THE WORLD YOUR RUNWAY

When you're trying to defeat depression and suicide, one of the most valuable things you can do is focus in on what you do have: your family, your friends, people who care about you. Your job, regardless if it's your dream job or not, your talents, abilities, & strengths. All the positives in your life. We have to make a habit of not focusing on our negative attributes or the negative things in our lives at the moment. We have to realize the situation can and will get better.

Everyone has been through a rough patch in life: broken hearts, failed relationships, loss of jobs, loss of loved ones, rejection, loneliness, fear, being bullied, wanting to fit in, being misunderstood or taken for granted. What life has taught me is that we have to take what we have and make the most out of it. If you have a dream to help people or you want to be a rapper or you want to model or dance or write a novel, whatever the dream is in your heart, pursue it.

Being successful doesn't always mean you have to have a large platform, a lot of money, or everyone in your corner. Following your dreams is following your heart into your destiny. Pursuing something you dream about gives you purpose in life. It motivates you. It inspires. Use your gifts and talents to be a blessing to others, even if you don't get the limelight or celebrity status. I guarantee you will enjoy the journey of your pursuit of happiness. I've always wanted to be a model ever since I was about five years old. I would put on different outfits and pose in the mirror, and I will walk down the hallway as if I was walking down the red carpet, and that dream stuck with me. When I was in first grade, the teacher asked me, "What do you want to be when you grow up?" and I said I wanted to be a beautiful model. She smiled as if she believed I could do it. Her smile gave me hope.

What I have realized over my lifetime is that nothing goes according to plan. The hardships of life things can get in the way, discourage you and make you feel defeated. I had to look at the bright side. I had to work regular jobs. I had to work side jobs just to make a living, pay bills, and take care of my daughter. Reality can be so discouraging at times, but I held onto my dream, and today I am modeling. Not on a large platform, not in major magazines, and I don't make a lot of money, but yet and still I hope it is possible, and I have had an amazing time in my pursuit of modeling. I have traveled to different places in different parts of the world. I've taken beautiful photos. I've done charity events and I have had such a wonderful time.

So even if you don't make it big, still try to be creative, make the world your runway, and have a good time being positive because you'll never know if you don't ever try.

LIFE IS A BATTLE YOU CAN WIN

Life is full of ups and downs. We all know this, but sometimes it can be so frustrating to be overwhelmed with the pressures of everyday life, and how nothing goes your way. There always seems to be something else to deal with.

When I was a child, I was bullied for my hair, the way that I looked, being overweight, my skin color, and my teeth. I got called "piranha mouth," ugly, fat, stupid, and worthless. Everything you could think of. It was harsh. I know young people today are suffering from bullies and insecurity and so many self-esteem issues, because they're not only being ridiculed in school, they're being ridiculed publicly through social media for the entire world to see. On public display for millions and thousands to ridicule them.

This is a kind of pressure many people who grew up in the 80s and 90s did not have to deal with. It's a whole 'nother world, with cyber bullies and just bullying in general. The fact you can see the negativity someone posts about you or says about you, and you can have so many people being negative toward you all at one time can be too much. We sometimes feel like the entire world is against us. This is a horrible feeling, and the Internet won't ever let you forget your failures.

So today's generation is definitely under a kind of pressure their parents may not understand. We have to fight for ourselves, for our lives, and our God-given right to live and to be happy. People take advantage of others and don't seem to care about the major emotional trauma they cause by being insensitive bigots. This type of abuse is wrong on so many levels and it's not taken seriously enough to bring about change. You do not have to put up with abuse of any form or any kind.

I know life can be overwhelming, but you have a purpose, just by the fact you are **breathing**. The fact you are on this earth is proof enough there is a purpose for your life. I remember watching the movie ***Captain Marvel***, and feeling empowered. Near the climax, Carol Danvers (Captain Marvel) was bound and unable to move. The enemy was mentally trying to break her and basically told her she could not break free, she was not strong enough. Captain Marvel recalled every moment in her life where she had been knocked down when she was about five or six years old, in a race car that basically blew up and she walked away: when she fell down, she got back up. While training she fell from the rope, she stood tall and got back up. When she was a child playing baseball and fell to the ground she got back up. The lesson in that movie for me, and for so many of us: *Life will knock us down, but we have to get back up. We have to stand tall and say, "No, I will not let this defeat me. I will not allow this to be the end for me. I will persevere. I will get through this."* And as she recalled all those moments where she got back up and tried again, she realized her strength, and she eventually broke free of the mental chains and the physical bonds. She was stronger than she even knew.

That's what we have to realize about ourselves: we are stronger than we realize. We have the capacity and ability to get through anything that comes against us in this life. If there is a problem, there is also a solution. If there is a negative, there is also a positive. So we have to recognize that we do not have to stand alone in silence, in fear and isolation, or in pain. We can get up when we fall down. We can get up when we're knocked down. We can get up when there are mental strongholds from people beating up on our self-esteem. We can get up from anything coming against us in our lives. We can choose to be more than what people expect. We can choose to be more than we even expected of ourselves.

You have the strength. You just have to tap into it. **Get Up, Get Up, Get Up**! Don't stay defeated, don't stay down, don't believe the lies, don't believe the hype, don't receive the negativity coming against you. Remember: If there is a problem in your life, there is also a solution.

You are not alone. You have friends, you have family, you have people who will back you up. You have someone, and even if you don't have anyone you have yourself. You have all the capabilities you will ever need. Your first step is to get back up and try again. Refuse to accept negativity and keep pushing forward. You got this!

POWERLESS OR POWERFUL

Powerless or powerful? What will we choose in our everyday life? I was recently inspired by Julia Fowler, I actually was on social media and came across her post on instagram @juliaafowler. She is an inspiring woman who has overcome such a huge struggle with losing weight and dieting. She's lost over 200lbs. She said something so interesting: *"We have a choice every day"!* "A choice to make good decisions. A choice to make negative decisions" (2019). For Julia Fowler, it was bad eating habits, eating fast food and sweets, choices that caused her to become overweight, but she tapped into something in herself to want change.

Julia inspires me. I love to hear stories of people overcoming battles with difficult situations. These stories are reminders of hope and change. I struggle with my own diet. I know how hard it can be to maintain your weight, to fight your cravings and just make good decisions, because we are emotional creatures. Sometimes we want to make the right decisions, but the day can cause us to be in a certain mood; a happy, celebrating mood, or a depressed, sad mood, even a frustrated or angry mood. We can make split-second decisions without even thinking.

Sometimes we can't shake them, the temptations are too great. We can't shake the feelings, we can't shake the negativity.

Emotionally weak at the moment, we lash out or we act on impulse. So it's not easy and simple, just making the right decision. So many other elements in our lives and around us influence our decisions. Julia made an excellent point about being powerful or powerless, or powerless regarding your habits, bad choices and decisions, powerless in a victim mentality. Powerless to act on the fact that you have a choice and you can make a change, even if it's difficult. You **can** choose to be powerful. Don't accept negativity. Make positive strides in your decision making and be all you can be. Take the right steps and move in the right direction, even if it's an inch at a time.

Take back your life. Make choices that make an impact and empower you. This relates to depression and suicidal thoughts for so many people, the choices we make and the things we allow in our lives, our hearts, our minds, our thoughts, everything. We have to realize we have a choice. We can choose to accept the negative thoughts, or negative feelings about ourselves, about our loved ones, about our circumstance, or we can choose to think positively even when times seem hopeless.

So many people are suffering with depression because of maybe a job situation, loss of a loved one, a break-up, a death in the family, a sexual assault, weight problems, health problems, money, family issues, bullying, feeling worthless, shame, guilt, making so many mistakes, etc. Regardless of the reason for your depression or suicidal thoughts, you need to recognize you are still in control. You have the ability to make a choice. A choice with your thoughts, a choice with your life and what you do next.

Suicide is a choice, but it's a choice that is final. There is no more room for improvement or growth because death is final. **Suicide doesn't end suffering, it ends your life. It ends your possibilities and**

every opportunity to be who you really are. It robs you of the chance to make things right, to heal and to grow.

Be powerful. Make a choice that is hopeful, positive, beneficial, productive, empowering, and inspiring. You are powerful. Someone needs to hear your story. Someone needs you! You are never alone in your struggles. Someone else has a story similar to yours, and if they can get through it, you can get through it too.

HAVING HOPE IN HOPELESSNESS

There is hope in hopelessness.

First of all, I want to say I am nobody, just someone who's suffered all my life with extreme obstacles. Someone who can relate to depression, to thoughts of suicide, and every bit of hopelessness that depression can bring on your life. Even if these are only short-lived, spare moments in your life where you feel down and out. You're back to your old self eventually, though, even in times where the depression lasts for months and sometimes even years on end. My entire goal by sharing my story, sharing my progress, letting you into my life and all of its details and disappointments, is to help someone out there who is at the end of their rope, who feels like life isn't worth living, who wants to give up, who has lost all the fight in them to live and survive

I'm speaking to the individuals who are truly hurt and need healing mentally, physically, and emotionally. I've been there, and I'm here to tell you it gets better.

Feeling broken. When something goes wrong, if someone breaks your heart, when you don't get a job opportunity, or you just are not where you expected to be in life. Or maybe you're having constant chaos, with problems hitting you in the face back-to-back. You seem to never get a break from anything. Then you have people tell you to get over it. It's no big deal. Why are you upset? You're procrastinating. You're lazy. You're just not working hard enough. As if it's that simple to just move on, feel better, be happy and joyous?

Sometimes the depression hits you when you wake up, or in the middle of the day, or right before you go to bed. Sometimes you wake up feeling energetic, hopeful, and better. Then other days you feel lost, hopeless, drained, exhausted, wondering where you went wrong and why you are even still here. It's almost as if in those moments, your very existence is pointless.

The hopelessness, the hurt, the pain, the depression itself keep you stuck. You can't seem to get out of bed. You have no motivation. You're sad. You lack energy to do even the basics. It's a struggle to get into the shower, to eat, to brush your hair, to go to work, to go to school, to deal with your everyday chores. It's like being paralyzed from sadness. Nobody quite gets it, nobody else really understands, so you do your best to hide it and push yourself and drag yourself to work or school, trying your best to keep up your everyday routine.

Sometimes in those moments you feel a little relief, a little smile, a little peace, but the hopelessness always creeps back in. From my own experience with depression, I believe it resulted from a lifetime of continuous tragedy, disappointments, unmet expectations, hurt, heartbreak, pain, chaos, confusion, death, family problems, and broken relationships.

I grew up poor in a young family. Poverty comes with its own kind of depression. Lacking basic resources, education, and food can give anyone depression. When you're a kid you're full of wonder, of hope, of dreams and ambitions. When life constantly kicks you down, you slowly see those hopes and ambitions start to disappear. It's easy to say, "Just work hard.

Just go to school. Just get a good education. Just do your best. Just keep pushing, keep striving, you'll be successful, you'll get things accomplished." Especially when the person telling you this is someone who has no idea what you're going through mentally, physically, or financially. Most of the time it is easier said than done. With all of the pressures of the world today, especially for young people trying to be popular, beautiful, and trendy, with all the superficial materialism, it's easy to lose sight of what's important. You start to beat yourself up mentally for not measuring up to someone else's ideals.

My childhood was about survival, not about toys and games or having fun or going out. It was about hoping to have enough food to eat, being there for my family. Many times, children from impoverished families don't understand why they can't do what other children do, or have what other people have. All they know is what they see and how they feel from their own experience, which isn't much. It's easy for a child in this kind of condition to feel left out, alone, and hopeless.

I remember as a child not having very much, but being happy. I saw my mother working hard to take care of us, and loving her so much. I remember thinking my mother was the most beautiful girl in the world, when I was young. It didn't matter how little we had, it was about having each other. It wasn't until I got older, when I had an understanding of what being poor was, that my feelings about my life changed. In elementary school I had a difficult time, mostly because of a teacher. I'll never forget her. Mrs. Sharp was Caucasian and I was in the third grade. I didn't know what racism was until I met her. It hurts to be treated badly because of the color of your skin, because of the race you come from, something you have no control over, something you shouldn't be mistreated for. I barely learned anything in her class. All of the black students in my class would get mistreated by her. She called us monkeys and ugly stupid hoes. At eight years old, hearing some names and terms I wasn't even familiar with, I still knew something was wrong. I just didn't know what, and I always felt so bad. She would tell me I was cute, but the other black girls were ugly. I didn't think they were ugly. And even in her complimenting me, I felt bad.

This was the beginning of my self-esteem issues. I eventually told my mother about this teacher and I was removed from her class, but the damage was already done.

My life during this time felt as if something was chasing me. I was at war and something invisible I could not see was after me, trying to destroy me, trying to take my life, steal my hope and all my dreams.

Not only was I pregnant and then a teen mother and trying to finish high school, but as I related earlier, I was stalked by the man who sexually assaulted me. I couldn't catch a break. Plus, everyone thought I got pregnant because I was easy or fast or just irresponsible.

I didn't dare tell anyone what really happened. Even mentioning it now bothers me, how it reflects on me, my family, and my child, but this isn't their story to tell, it's mine. In my sophomore year I was really looking forward to singing in the school choir, but my choir teacher told me it didn't look good for me to represent the school while I was pregnant, so I had to sit this one out. Of course I was heartbroken, another thing taken from me, yet I pushed forward and stayed positive

I looked forward to meeting my child and vowed to be a really good mom and love her unconditionally, and not hold anything against her. First and foremost, she was mine, and if I could not have all my dreams come true, my new dream would be her and I would make sure no one hurt her like the world has hurt me.

Because I was being stalked by my abuser in high school, and because the restraining order did little good, I went to Job Corps in Charleston, West Virginia, to get away from him and complete my high school diploma. During that time, I earned some business college credits. When I returned home, I got together with a few of my friends from high school and elementary school who I had known for many years. They were heavily involved with drugs and drinking. I had always felt that wasn't good for them, but they wouldn't listen to me. Growing up, I never did see the appeal of drinking and smoking, so I didn't get involved with it. I was teased about being afraid and not trying new things, but that didn't bother me.

so many unfortunate events occurred in my life that I had to constantly struggle against all odds against, that pushed me in directions I normally wouldn't have gone if something different had happened.

I met someone else at the age of eighteen. He was sweet and kind at first. We were both young. I knew I couldn't be my age. I always had to be more responsible, mature, and make sure I was there for my daughter. There was no time for partying, drinking or taking drugs. I had to figure out how I was going to support my child and maintain a life for us. My life was about survival. I really couldn't be a teenager and have fun. I had to push through the pain and get things done. It wasn't about me anymore or what I suffered through. It became about her not suffering.

He asked me to marry him on his computer screen in the living room of his apartment. I found that a little odd, but I knew he was nervous and a little shy at times, so I didn't hold it against him. I loved him, so I said yes. We were married around my twentieth birthday. He moved into my small apartment and I thought everything would be fine. We got along with each other and we cared about each other, so that was all we needed. I didn't know at the time he only married me for the extra military allotment money, to pursue his own goals outside of me and my daughter. I found out all this later, plus the fact he had another apartment with another woman, after I quit my job to go to business school full-time. Despite the troubles his actions caused me, I graduated with honors on the National Dean's List.

My husband's lies and betrayal put me in a financial bind because he had stopped helping with bills. As I said earlier in this book, I had a hard time finding work to let me finish school and support my daughter. One of my few options was to become a dancer. It was a very hard decision to make. I didn't think I was very pretty, but maybe I was pretty enough to make a few dollars to get by. At this time I was twenty-four years old. The world of exotic dance is chaotic, confusing, and intimidating. I was so shy and timid, it's amazing to me how I got past my stage fright to even perform. I didn't take drugs or drink alcohol to put myself in a mood, to try to zone out while I was dancing on stage. I just waited for my favorite song and danced like no one else was watching. I would think about the things I wanted to do for myself and my daughter, trips we would take. I let the thought of her motivate me to keep trying and to stay positive.

Dancing at a go-go bar was never my dream job or something I even imagined myself having to do or even needing to do. I always felt bad for working there because of all of the moral stigmas and all the negative things people would say about girls who worked in that kind of industry. It's tabu. It's the sex industry. So I decided to just use this as a stepping stone to get ahead and get something else going for myself.

Planning for my life was never that simple, because just like in my childhood, chaos and trouble seemed to be chasing me to keep me from having many options and or choices. I feel like I've always been between a rock and a hard place and backed into a corner. Even though my situation seemed to be a hopeless case of unfortunate events and many setbacks, I hung on to God's word. I decided to not let my obstacles stop me from being the best person I could be.

I learned so much about myself and about other people. I was placing way too much trust in so-called friends and not enough trust in God. I knew if I continued to make decisions out of impulse, I would only dig a deeper hole for myself. I'm thankful that with all the negative things that have happened in my life, I kept seeking the Lord for help.

Some may be able to relate to the betrayal I've experienced or the heartbreak of trusting a friend, believing someone loved you and finding out they never did. This type of misfortune leaves people in a depressive state of mind. It's hard to see a bright side when every turn in life seems to be something else that knocks you down.

I remember when I started the LifeLine program and how so many people reached out and wanted to be involved. I had many friends from Facebook donate and support me. Unfortunately, a few people were skeptical of my motives and intentions. It really broke my heart that a few people tried to belittle my cause dealing with depression and suicide. When I started LifeLine Project Your Life Matters, Defeating Depression and Teens and Young Adults, no one really knew why I decided to start this program.

The truth: my daughter was suffering, and I've always had a heart for people who were depressed and suicidal because I have suffered a great deal of tragedy that left me hopeless, to the point of not wanting to live or even try.

When I saw my daughter between the age of thirteen and sixteen suffering, constantly feeling like life was pointless, I had to do something. What I decided to do was to lift her out of despair, along with other young people like her and adults who needed my testimony, my care, and devotion to this cause.

I am typing this with tears in my eyes, because I can't imagine my life without her. I cry for every parent who has lost a child to suicide. I cry for their loss and their helplessness from not knowing what to do. I hurt for every person who feels lost, alone, ashamed, and heartbroken. I know how horrible it can feel to want to die and not want anyone to know, yet at the same time wanting them to be there and see that you're hurting, without directly saying it.

My daughter was going through so much from the things she experienced in school, and she tried to handle it all on her own. Things eventually came to the surface and I found out everything going on at her school. It's a shame how other kids can be so heartless and cruel, and they convince their victims that if they tell, things will only get worse. The more they keep the secret, the worse things get. This experience with my daughter taught me to always watch for signs in her behavior to know if there is something wrong, things that maybe she isn't comfortable telling me.

To see my daughter struggle with depression and suicide made me realize how much there is lacking in mental health help for our kids and adults. I created a program for kids and young adults from the ages of eight to twenty-one. Even one life saved is a victory in my eyes.

I appreciate Lifeline National Hotline and also Teenline Online Teens helping Teens. These resources are amazing and so helpful to teens and adults. I decided I wanted to add an additional resource of encouragement for youth and anyone suffering with depression and suicidal thoughts. I realized that even though I'm only one person, my care and positive energy most likely can help someone.

During the time I started doing events at different locations, such as Buffalo Wild Wings, Dave & Busters and IHop, my modeling started to take off, so I decided to do both. My heart was still there and I continued to stay very involved in helping young people and adults out of depression. In this program, they could be enrolled to get Lifeline and Teenline information, and other resources in their local area. I set up a Go Fund Me account where I received donations to help with events and also to help give each child and young adult a gift card. This program is something I wanted to do to reassure the kids and young people that they are not alone. It's a small gesture of love and encouragement to them.

I appreciate the people who have helped and supported this cause. I'm very thankful for the support I have received. The negative people who assumed the worst about me kind of sunk me back into a place of feeling like maybe what I was trying to do was too big and I wouldn't be able to make a positive impact. It hurts when people try to knock you down and don't give you an opportunity to show them your genuine intent.

As an adult, I'm still being bullied and talked down to and talked about, but I've come too far to stop now. So I say to the negative people who don't think I have good intentions: You're wrong, and all the kids and teens and young adults will testify to my intentions, because I am determined to help as many people as possible out of treacherous despair. I can be a model and a role model against depression and suicide. I can be courageous in my pursuit of positive change in the mindset of hurting people.

I want to reach my goals and show other people who have been hurt and depressed like me and my daughter. You can be hopeful, and you can be more than the negative things you may be feeling, or the negative things people are saying to you. My passion is healing the brokenhearted and letting others know they're not alone in this. If no one else is with you, Jesus is, and I'm a living witness to the change that God can bring.

TRAGEDIES AND TRIUMPH

I can tell you all day how many tragedies I've had in my life, but I also need to tell you about my triumphs and my victories, about times when I didn't know how I was going to make it or what was coming next, and I was blessed. Life is full of ups and downs, unexpected tragedy, little moments where you laugh until your sides hurt, and other moments where you cry yourself to sleep. But through it all, you have to see the good, the positive side, the light in your life. At times things can get so bad you can't see any good and you don't feel like it could ever get better, but you have to realize it can't always rain. The sun has to shine eventually. That basically means this may be a down time for you, but just hang in there. Something good, some light will be shining through for you

Don't give up, don't give in. This is what life is about: constantly persevering against every obstacle and all odds. This life is a challenge, and it has so much meaning and purpose. It's your responsibility to find out what your meaning and purpose are. So many people miss the opportunity to discover themselves because they don't feel they have a purpose, they don't realize what life is all about, and they don't ever take the time to discover it. The truth is, without God there is no hope.

Some people who lack faith are constantly striving to have more money, to improve their self-image and their life's meaning and purpose. All of those things are fine, but if you don't have something of substance driving you to keep pushing forward, you will eventually burn yourself out and the logic of staying alive will increasingly become pointless. Some people believe that faith in God is just some comforting tool to get you through hard times, to help you feel more important because you don't have much else. The truth is, having faith is much deeper than that. It's so much more. You have to get to know who God is, why He sent His son to die on the cross for our sins, and our need for a Savior. ***God so loved the world that he gave his only begotten son so that whoever believes in him would not perish but have everlasting life. John 3:16***

FAITH

To a person who knows little about the gospel, there are so many unanswered questions about Jesus and everything involved with Christianity. Some people feel it's complete nonsense or untruth and it's not relatable to anything real. **The bigger picture is, if it's not true, you have nothing to lose, but if it is true you have everything to lose and yet so much to gain.** The gospel is God's free gift of salvation. Grace is given to you freely by faith in Jesus. It is not about what you have done or will ever do.

God changes you and gives you a new heart capable of love, capable of change, capable of breaking bad habits. With what I do know about the Lord, you definitely don't want to miss your blessings in this life or the next. **You don't want to miss out on miracles.** Some people say, "Well, what does God have to do with depression and why do I have to believe in God to get over my depression?" Well why not? If nothing else in your life is helping, why not consider the gospel? You're looking and searching for **purpose**.

Why not try something different that may open your eyes to something bigger than yourself? No matter what you do, there will be people who oppose it because they don't care, they don't need it, they don't understand, and that's their right. You don't have to accept what I'm saying. You don't have to believe, but it's definitely something you should consider if you are exhausted with life, exhausted from pain and problems.

Jesus is much more than comfort. He is peace, He is hope, He is love everlasting. He is the living word. A relationship with Jesus Christ is not another religious set of rules and regulations. When you accept Jesus Christ into your life, you are changed from the inside out, your heart is changed, your mind is changed, that empty void in the depths of your soul finally is filled with joy, peace and love, and yes, you will have human moments. Becoming a Christian is not about sitting in church and pretending to be perfect or judging others. It is about accepting the free gift of salvation that the Lord has given us through His Son **Jesus Christ.** When you have the Lord in your life, it's an indescribable feeling you only can experience through accepting Him. I have found other religions promise peace and joy, but none of them speak of salvation or deliverance, redemption, everlasting life, or forgiveness of sin.

When I heard the gospel for the first time, everything inside of me, my heart, my spirit and my soul, felt this overwhelming, inspiring sensation of truth. Only the gospel has given me that. It was much more than an inspirational message, it was much more than encouraging. It was much more than some lecture or speech or hope or something to confide in that would make my life better. This was the meaning of the word **truth** I found in Christ Jesus, a complete knowing in the depths of my soul that this is the absolute truth. This is authentic, genuine love in its purest form. My life was forever changed. I still have obstacles and struggles, but the biggest difference is that I have a peace that surpasses my pain from the past and the present, and no kind of medicine prescription therapy has given me that.

By all means, if you need therapy or even medication or to be under a doctor's care, please do so. I also recommend alongside that a dose of Jesus, a dose of the Gospel, a dose of the word of God, and a dose of faith. Once I accepted Jesus as my Lord and Savior, I started to study and I started to understand what all of this meant, what the gospel actually was. **The gospel is the most beautiful, amazing expression of God's love for mankind, a solidifying revelation of sacrifice and commitment.**

In school, they teach us that Darwin's theory of evolution is what happened in the world and that's how all living cells and organisms came about. It's funny how we as people don't question that theory as much as we question God's existence. As complex as the human body is, and every planet in the universe is different and unique, along with every creature on land and in the sea, our very existence has to be more than just something that happened. It has to be deeper than that. Sometimes we dismiss obvious truths that are staring us right in the face.

Most of the time when it comes to Jesus, there's resistance and negativity. Why is the gospel so offensive? But hate and discrimination are not?

Pay attention to things the entire world wants to shut down and shut out. Most of the time, that's where the truth is hidden. Life isn't all about getting stuff and surpassing others' materialistic gain. It has a deeper, more profound meaning and purpose. You need to know the truth to be set free, to realize why you matter, why you're here and what you're supposed to do. Life isn't all about followers and likes and popularity, being rich, having the most fancy car and clothing, or being the most beautiful.

Life has such more meaning than the world will express or even say. We get caught up in popularity contests, trying to outdo the next person, when the only one we should be competing with is our former selves. We have a responsibility to discover who we are and what we need to do in our own individual lives. No wonder people are depressed and feel inadequate. They're trying to constantly measure up to other people's lives that are not their own.

You can't compare an apple to an orange, and you have no business trying to compete where you don't compare. Your life is your own and you have your own unique set of qualities and distinctions. We have to realize this life is not a rat race, to beat someone else. We measure our self-worth based on materialism, based on where we come from, how much money we have, where we live and the car we drive. Your value in the kingdom of God is based on His love for you. This life is a journey. It's okay to be who you are. Set your own trends even if they're not popular or other people don't like them. You have a right to be unique and different. You were not created to fit in, but to stand out. No two people on the earth are exactly alike. Even identical twins have different sets of fingerprints and different personalities. We were designed on purpose, for a purpose. Discover who you are as an individual, instead of trying to measure up to your peers or celebrities or other people.

We all have unique gifts and talents. It's time for you to find yourself and reach your full potential. It's hard to live life to your full potential when you're afraid, you doubt, you don't believe in yourself, or you don't have people in your corner to support you. I definitely understand this, and God has given me the support, the faith, and the fearlessness I needed to move forward in life. I have hope even though I'm not wealthy.

Life is about learning and progress. I definitely understand struggles and how some people have privileges while others have nothing at all. I definitely understand pain, abuse, frustrations, and suffering. With all of this negativity, it's hard to believe there is a God, a loving God who would allow all of these things to happen and that it's possible to have peace with all these problems. This is why it is so very important that you read and discover and understand what the scriptures have to say and find out what the gospel actually is.

Find out why the Lord has allowed this suffering, and why there is an appointed time for it to end. If you don't tap into who created you and gave you this life, you will end up missing the whole point of your very existence. Read for yourself, discover the truth. Don't take anyone's word for it.

One thing I definitely can say: my life has changed for the better. I have seen miracles and I have seen blessings and I have seen how things have worked out for me when no other way could have been possible. Divine favor! Divine intervention! It feels good not to worry and stress all the time, even though my circumstances are not where I want them to be. I see that I have grace, I have mercy, and I have peace that I didn't have before.

GRATITUDE

You are the sweetest song, the kindest friend, the most loving Father. **A Lord who is above all, yet humble, pure and true. Your beauty surpasses all understanding Your love is more abundant than anyone can comprehend.** You are my secret place of comfort and a peace this world does not give. Lord, in Your presence all sorrow is left behind. Sometimes I just want to escape and go home. A home that is not on this planet. A place that surpasses time and every dimension. Patiently, I wait for You. I know there is much work to do, but in the moments when I rest and I'm in deep thought, I think of You, Your mysterious plans and how everything is coming together. How You are making everything new.

Truly You are wondrous and amazing. Even though I don't know all there is to come, I trust You. I am waiting for You and I know You will come for me. I anticipate the day, I am longing for the moment. I'm eager to see, but in the meanwhile, I will have faith. I will push through. **I will fight the good fight of faith.** I will do the work You have on earth for me. I will trust You. I'll wait on You. In Your loving kindness You take care of me. You comfort my soul and I'm so thankful. You are my everlasting hope.

You are happiness, joy and kindness, generosity, charity and helpfulness, innocence, purity and holiness. These are qualities I want over my life. I want righteousness in my life. I want goodness and mercy. I know sometimes my childlike heart gets me in trouble and maybe I should have done away with my naive ways long ago, but I know You are with me, protecting me from even my own self, my own foolish decisions.

Bless me through healing and forgiveness. Bless me with goodness. The kind of goodness that causes people to want to change and help others. The kind of goodness that makes a difference, that undoes the evil of the world. The Holy Spirit has placed in me encouragement, inspiration, devotion, loyalty, kindness, care, and courage. Develop me in all of these areas of righteousness, purity, holiness, and truth. I don't want to be in sin, vanity, lust or lies. **Develop me into Your true beauty. The kind of beauty that eyes cannot see and hands cannot hold.**

I'm not deserving of Your kindness or Your love, but You shower it on me daily. Help me not to get selfish and take advantage of Your kindness and Your mercy. Help me, Lord, in the areas I am weak. You know I'm in this body, I am limited in myself, but with You all things are possible. I believe You are going to do amazing things in my life that I could never even imagine. Bless me with wisdom. Mold me, renew me, and finish the work You have started in my life. In Jesus' name. Amen.

This is a personal letter and prayer to God from my heart. I encourage you to pray about your future and show your gratitude towards Jesus, because if He has given me this much hope with everything I have been through, I know He has something amazing for you as well! Just believe! Have Faith.

ARE YOU JUST EXISTING?

Have you ever just been tired of existing? Do you ever just feel exhausted with life, with getting up in the morning routine? Do you ever feel like the ultimate rest would be to leave all of this behind, every single bit of it? Have you ever felt just so tired, not just of a job, school or things going wrong or negative people, but everything: brushing your teeth, getting out of bed, watching TV, going to work, eating, bills, going out, the stress? Then you have a small ray of sunshine in your life, a good moment, only to be devastated by something negative and feel like the darkest, heaviest clouds are drifting over you and knock you back so far. Have you ever been completely sick and tired of struggling? Of trying to comprehend, *Why is this constantly happening to me?*

What is the purpose of it all? What's the point to keep fighting if my struggle is never-ending? If I'm only walking in circles and my suffering is inevitable. Do my family and friends really need me? Is it possible I'm this waste of space that can never get it right? What is the point if I accomplish one thing and not master another? If all of my efforts will not keep me from being at this low? Why should I go on when family and friends cause me to feel as if I'm useless or use me up without any regard for how I feel? **The very thing I want out of life seems to be out of my reach.** A constant reminder and torturous memory, all wrapped in one. If my fate is to constantly be at war with life's complications, why should I keep fighting? Answer: *Simply because you are worth fighting for!* It's very true that life is an ongoing struggle with plenty of ups and downs. Sometimes in life it seems like you have more bad days than good. This is true. But **we have to remember with everything happening to us and around us in life, it will not last forever.** I think we all get sick and tired of this repetitive struggle and opposition. *The truth is, life gets better and worse all at the same time.* **Our perceptions can either heighten the negativity or diminish it**, when we're at our lowest point and feel like giving up, feeling like maybe giving up would be so much better than enduring one more agonizing moment in the mental pain and anguish we're suffering right now.

But the truth is, when you think about the people you love, the things you want to accomplish, even thinking about others who may feel similar to you, that can cause you to realize you have a purpose.. At my lowest point in life, when I thought about other people and how it really hurts to know I'm feeling like this, knowing someone else may be experiencing this or something way worse caused me to want to do something about it..

It allowed me to get my mind off my problems and how I felt, and I started focusing on how someone else may be feeling. This thought made me realize that when we're at our lowest point and are only thinking about ourselves and how we feel, without any regard for the people around us, we can't see our purpose outside of our own pain. I realized it's not good for me to focus on all the negativity about myself, about my circumstances, about my family. When I focus on the negative so deeply, of course dying seems like the best solution, but it's not.

I didn't even consider anything else, I was only thinking about myself and the way I was feeling and what I was dealing with and what I wanted and what I couldn't have. It was all about me and nothing and no one else. **Life's biggest purpose is how you affect other people's lives. Our lives are not just about us and what we want.** We are connected to people, to others, to our family, to our friends, to our spouses, to our siblings, our cousins, classmates, coworkers. **This journey is not all about us, and when we take time to recognize this truth, we may tap into what we can do to resolve the pain within ourselves and others.**

Try this today: think about your family, someone you know has tried to help you and cared about you and showed some kind of concern. Think of the classmate who stood up for you, or that teacher who made a difference, that friend who always has something good to say, the person at the grocery store who genuinely smiled at you and was happy to see you. These small instances are enough rays of hope to help you realize there is some positivity in this world for you to value your life.

I truly believe love heals all wounds. Love yourself, be patient with yourself, love other people, have compassion, take it easy and don't give yourself such a hard time. No one is perfect. Failure is an opportunity to learn, so don't beat yourself up about making a mistake. **Mistakes can be fixed. Problems can be solved. Death is final.** We should not resort to death over temporary problems. You can get through this.

You're important, you're special, you're unique, you are different, and if you give yourself a chance and some time, you will be amazed by what you'll accomplish. Even a small step in the right direction is still moving forward. You got this!

CHOOSE LIFE

We should ask ourselves: What will we live for today? Every day in life, we should ask ourselves: What are we living for? What are we striving for? And who is affected by our very existence? Are these people important to me? Once we realize our lives are not all about us and stop being selfish about what we want, what we think, and what we need, and we consider our loved ones and consider the people who count on us every day, we won't have time to feel as if we don't have a purpose. Mental health is not made up of just feelings, emotions, inadequacies and failures. It's also made up of health, diet, sleep patterns, and balance.

We need balance. We need proper rest. We need a good diet. We need to have peace, love, and joy. When we're lacking in one area or another, the body doesn't adjust well. It doesn't function as it should. So life is not all about just caring for others, it's also about caring for yourself as well. Taking the time to adjust yourself and realize what you need if you're lacking in rest and sleep. My depression made it very difficult to sleep. My body would be at rest, but my mind would be racing. Moments like this, I needed to stay calm and relax. I recommend nighttime tea such as Sleepy Time Celestial Seasonings. It's an all-natural tea made with calming herbs like valerian root and chamomile.

Take time to ask yourself who or what is causing you pain, anguish or stress. Who in my life is adding to my health and adding value to my life? Take time to do a process of eliminating foods from your diet that are harming you, along with negative friendships. Resolve family issues that may be weighing heavy on your mind and heart. When we're stressed and not eating right and not sleeping like we should, of course the brain will be out of whack.

There will be imbalances that only add to the problems you already have. In society today, we are workaholics. We have little time to think or to take care of ourselves. We are constantly on the go, almost forced to eat fast food and making poor choices with our diet from the lack of time or the lack of time management or the lack of caring about nutrition and health. Whatever the reason, it's definitely time to take a step back and fix whatever may be causing these deep-rooted issues.. We are very complex, different individuals. The Lord has made all of us very unique and very different. Some people can eat certain foods and not have a problem, while others can't function with the same diet.

This is why it's so important that you find out what works for you. What foods work for you, what work environments work for you, and what sleep pattern works for you. Trying to live in someone else's mold will drain all of your energy. Trying to force yourself to fit in an environment or situation that isn't for you will cause you tremendous psychological, physical, emotional, and mental damage.

What Jesus has done for me is help me weed out the unnecessary elements in my life that don't better me as a person and as an individual. The Lord gives me divine wisdom in the areas of my health, my emotional health, my physical health, and my spiritual health. Faith allows you to have balance. Jesus has brought balance and order into my life, a realization and discovery of who I am and what works for me, things that make me happier as a person. He helps me become more productive. More outlets for creative thinking, and thinking outside of every problem that may arise in my life.

One thing is for sure, no matter what you have going on or what you believe in: you're going to have problems. Things are going to happen. You're going to have some kind of heartache and heartbreak. Something's not going to be completely right, and we have to find a coping mechanism to get through these times. One for me is to be thankful every day. Be thankful for waking up. Wake up thankful, wake up inspired, because you never know what is waiting to try to knock you down and destroy your peace. We have to get to a point where we are not destroyed by every negative occurrence in our lives.

Expect good and bad and be hopeful for the best. We have to fight mentally and have a warrior's spirit toward life. We can't give up every time something doesn't go our way or something devastating happens. In these times, we have to see what we can do and push through the pain to get to the other side. Perseverance, creativity, love, and support will get us through life. We have to be able to have happiness and peace through it all. Be at peace. Jesus is the source for peace. Stay encouraged, stay positive, build up your endurance mentally and emotionally by putting faith into practice.

TRUE HAPPINESS

Life is difficult and no amount of attention, perfect circumstances, alcohol, drugs, likes, follows, views or sex can make a person whole inside. If you want to get rid of the depression and suicidal thoughts, get rid of the pain that causes you to keep drifting back and forth into this dark place mentally. You need God's help to bring order and healing over your mind.

Many think that taking their own lives is the only way out to stop hurt and pain, or avoid the frustrations of life. They can't see anything getting better, feeling as if maybe the entire world would be better off without them. Well, I'm here to tell you it *will* get better, you are needed, and even though you can't see it you have to make a decision to believe it anyway.

Your existence has meaning. Your family, friends and people who care about you need you around. Honestly, there are people you have never met that need you. I can say this with confidence, because I have personally experienced this. Your life is important and your presence can positively impact so many lives.

When you make a decision to just leave life, physically check out of life, you are disregarding everyone around you. You are robbing someone of your smile, your presence, your time, your energy. You have no idea the uplifting power you possess. I'm pretty sure if you asked around your office or your school, your neighborhood, family and friends, they could tell you many things about yourself that keep them inspired. Suicide is a form of abandonment. You are abandoning your life, your loved ones, your friends, your children, all your responsibilities and possibilities.

Pain and fear shouldn't stop you from reflecting on the damage that may be done from your absence. Whether you realize it or not, you have purpose and someone needs you. Many times in life, we give up too fast and too easily. It doesn't matter how many things have gone wrong in your life, how many mistakes you have made, there is a solution and room for improvement.

There is something that can be done. There is a solution to your problem. It is not hopeless. Nothing is final unless you believe it is. I want you to know, I care and even though I don't know you personally. I truly have a heart for you and what you are experiencing. I know how it feels to be alone and think no one cares, but it's not true. You have more people cheering for you then you even realize. I want to hear your story. I want to see you accomplish great things and even see you join me in this mission of saving lives! I want to have more events where all the survivors come together sharing their stories and how they have chosen life ! I stand with you forever and my hope is that you will see the miracles that will be manifested through your faith! Choose life!

Pray this prayer:

Lord, help me to have the strength to live everyday. Help me to cope with what is wrong in my life. Bring peace over the areas in my life I feel hopeless. Heal my heart and my pain. Send peace over my mind, over my thoughts, over my body. Allow me to sleep in peace and to awake in positive victory over every obstacle and problem in my life. In Jesus' name I pray. Amen.

WARNING SIGNS OF DEPRESSION

The warning signs to watch out for are:

- ✓ changes in weight or appetite,
- ✓ change in mood,
- ✓ sleeping more or less,
- ✓ drinking more than usual,
- ✓ mood changes,
- ✓ anxiety,
- ✓ acting more aggressively,
- ✓ making passing comments (or more) about death and dying,
- ✓ disengagement from people and activities that once were enjoyed,
- ✓ no longer seem to enjoy the things they used to,
- ✓ knowing someone who has tried suicide (Poland, 2020).

More than anything, trust that "feeling" you have that things aren't quite right. Always trust it.

If You Suspect Someone Is Thinking of Giving Up ...

If you think someone might be suicidal, ask the question. And be direct.

There's a misconception that discussing suicide might plant the idea, but it just doesn't work like this. If someone is contemplating suicide, the idea will already be there. If they aren't, talking about it won't put the idea into their mind. Suicide isn't caused by asking the question. Never has been.

One of the major causes of suicide are feelings of isolation and disconnectedness. People who are suicidal are hurting. Knowing that someone has cared enough to notice and ask the question can interrupt the path towards suicide enough for the person to seek help.

Be direct. To start with, try something like, 'You seem a bit down lately. Can we talk about it?' Then, if you suspect, even in the slightest, that the person might be suicidal, ask the question directly. "People who feel like that sometimes think about suicide. Do you have any thoughts of suicide?" Or just, "Are you thinking that you don't want to live anymore?"

Skirting around the issue by using words like "hurting yourself," instead of "suicide," can give the message that talking about suicide is unacceptable and might undermine the conversation. Suicidal people aren't interested in "hurting themselves," they're interested in killing themselves. An indirect question is less likely to bring about a direct response.

And If The Answer is "Yes"?

If the answer is "yes," take it seriously and don't minimize the situation with responses like, "Plenty of people feel like this but they don't kill themselves," or, "It's not that bad." If someone is thinking of killing themselves, it **is** that bad. It's as bad as it gets. What other people in the same situation did will be completely irrelevant.

Tell them you're there for them and you'll get through this together. Let them know depression is treatable and help them get help.

An important question in response to hearing someone is suicidal is to ask if the person has worked out how they would do it. If the answer is "I don't know," let them know you're there for them and help them get help. If the response reveals a clear intention to suicide and a plan, ask about the plan. Asking questions as though you were asking about a trip the person was going on: – where, when, how.

Most importantly, get help immediately. Call a national suicide support line or crisis line, take the person to a doctor or hospital, or if they won't go, call the doctor or hospital for help.

Above all, don't leave the person alone. Sometimes, if somebody has made the decision to suicide, they may seem happier than they have for a long time. This can be mistaken for a sign that the person has worked their way through to the other side of their depression and is feeling genuinely happier. What's more likely is that the happy change has come about because the person has found a way to end their hurt, and it will just be a matter of time. In this situation, stay vigilant, stay close and get help.

Talking about suicide is the surest way to keep safe those whose pain feels unbearable. It doesn't matter if the words you choose aren't the perfect ones. It's not about the words – it's about the connection, and anything said with compassion and a genuine intent will not do any harm (Websites, 2021; Young, 2021).

PRAYERS FOR PEACE AND FREEDOM

Ransomed Heart

Freedom comes only as we bring these unsanctified and unholy places under the rule of Jesus Christ, so He can possess these very places deeply and truly. Therefore, part of this first step involves sanctifying to Christ the place of bondage. If it's sexual, you sanctify your sexuality to Christ; if it's emotional (as with rage, or fear, or even grief), you sanctify your emotions; if it involves addiction, you sanctify your appetite, your obsession, and your body. At the retreats we do, we walk through this process in prayer, and many people are shocked to realize they have never taken the first, simple step of sanctifying their sexuality (or emotions, or appetites) to Jesus Christ. But if you want to be free in this place, it must come under the total, intimate, ongoing rule of God.

Lord Jesus, forgive me. I confess I have been offering myself over to sin, and now I am its slave. I renounce it; I renounce my sins.

[Be very specific here. For example, "I renounce the ways I have presented my sexuality to sin; I renounce my sexual sins. I present my sexuality to Jesus Christ. I sanctify my sexuality to Jesus Christ. I present the members of my body and my sexuality as instruments of righteousness. I renounce the ways I have presented my appetite and my drinking to sin; I renounce my sins with alcohol. I present my appetite and my drinking to Jesus Christ. I sanctify my body to Jesus Christ."]

> *I renounce every way I have given myself over to sin. I dedicate and I consecrate my life* [and this specific area] *once more to the rule of Jesus Christ, to be His and His alone. May Your atoning blood cover my sins and cleanse me. May Your holiness possess me totally and completely.*

You will also find it helpful to renounce the "sins of your fathers." Often in these places of lasting bondage, you will find that a father (or mother, or brother, or grandparent) struggled with the same issue. The scriptures present to us the reality that sin is often passed down within a family line, and the effects of those sins are also passed down generation to generation (see Ex. 20:5, 34:7, Lev. 26:39-42, Neh. 9:2).

> *Lord Jesus, I also renounce the sins of my fathers here* [or my mother, my grandmother, what have you]. *I renounce their sins of* [be specific, as in, "their rage, their sexual sins, their alcoholism."], *I utterly renounce and break with the sins of my family line. I plead the blood of Christ over those sins, so that they may not have a hold on me. I renounce them and break with them utterly.*

Breaking the Stronghold

We begin to break the enemy's hold on us through the presence of "agreements." By this I mean places in our own hearts that have made a deep agreement with a feeling, a thought, a sentence. If you have struggled with something for years now, there are probably agreements along the lines of: "I'll never get free of this," "I am such an $%#@," "Who cares anyway?" "It's too late," and a host of others.

Those are agreements, and they serve as a kind of permission for the enemy to keep you in bondage. So you must break them. In addition to these, there are the agreements with the sin itself: "I am filled with rage," "I am a drunk," "I am gay." They can even "feel" biblical but, friends, you do not want to be making agreements with your sin. You are dead to sin and alive to God. You are the dwelling place of Jesus Christ. You are forgiven and dearly loved. So you must break the agreements you've been making here, in this area. Some will be obvious to you; others require the presence of the Holy Spirit to reveal them.

> *Spirit of God, search me, know me, reveal to me the agreements I have been making in this area. I renounce those agreements now.* [Be very specific.] *I renounce the agreement that* [What is it? "I'll never get free?" "Rage is just a part of me?" "It's too late?"] *I break these agreements in the name of my Lord Jesus Christ. I renounce them. I renounce every claim they have given the enemy in my life. Jesus, my Deliverer, come and break these strongholds. Set me free in this very place.*

> *Lord Jesus, show me every companion agreement operating here. I renounce the agreement that I'm alone, that no one will protect me. I renounce the agreement that I am dirty and disgusting. I renounce every agreement with shame. I renounce the agreement that I can never be forgiven. Spirit, show me what to pray, reveal these agreements.*

This is how we undo that dynamic about letting the sun go down on these things and the enemy getting a foothold

(Eph. 4:26-27). Bit by bit you are recovering parts of your heart. You are taking them back from when you gave them away. This erodes the claim that you gave the enemy in your heart. Yes, terrible things may have happened to us, but we are the ones who made these agreements, these resolutions, these vows, and we're not going to see victory in that area until we renounce them.

I will be honest—if you've given your heart over to something many times over, you've given it a good stronghold, and if it is also tangled up in issues of wounds and sin, it's going to take some time to untangle and heal this, but it is worth the work. Don't just bury it. It's worth going into those dark places and those murky waters and working through it. The blood of Jesus Christ cleanses us of everything. Everything.

Having broken the agreements and renounced the sin, we often find that we have to be quite intentional in commanding the enemy to leave. "Submit therefore to God," wrote James the brother of Jesus, "resist the devil and he will flee from you" (Jms. 4:7). Much of what we have been doing up to this point is submitting to God, bringing these specific issues under the rule of Jesus by renouncing the sins, breaking the agreements, sanctifying these places back to the Lordship of Jesus Christ. Now comes part two of this verse: resist.

> *I bring the blood of my Lord Jesus Christ right here, in this very place. I renounce every claim I gave the evil one to my life right here, in this very place. And I bring the blood of Christ now against the strongholds and against the spirits operating here.* [Sometimes you will need to be firm and specific: I bring the blood of Jesus against all spirits of addiction, of alcoholism, all spirits of rage, of homosexuality, and so on]. *I banish these enemies from my life now—from my body, my soul, and my spirit. "Resist the devil and*

he will flee from you" (Jms. 4:7). I resist the devil here and now and I command these spirits to flee in the name of Jesus Christ my Lord.

Ask the Spirit to guide you. If you will stick with this and let the Holy Spirit guide you, you can be free.

Lord, forgive me for giving place in my heart to resentment, to lust, to anger, to alcohol. Forgive me for giving place in my life to resignation and self-reproach and shame, to fear and doubt and control. I renounce it now. Come, Jesus Christ, and take Your rightful place in my heart and in my life here. Come and set me free here, in these very places. I plead Your blood over these sins, and I break every hold I gave my enemy here, in the name of Jesus Christ.

As you do this, you erode your enemy's claims to keep you in bondage. By the way, your enemy is not going to like the fact that you are about to get free. He will try to discourage you from praying like this. He will try to distract you (the phone will ring, you'll suddenly be hungry, you'll feel like doing it tomorrow). He'll try to make you feel like, "This is so stupid, I can't believe I'm doing this out loud." He's going to make you feel like this isn't working or this isn't going to work, "Now I'm becoming one of those nuts." Just push through all of that.

I bring the work of Jesus Christ once more against you [shame, rage, fear, sexual sin, resignation, etc.] and I command you in the name of Jesus Christ to go to the throne of Jesus Christ in His mighty name. "It is for freedom that Christ has set you free" (Gal. 5:1). I claim my freedom now in the name of Jesus Christ. Jesus, I ask You to sanctify me through and through. May my whole spirit, soul, and body be kept blameless at the coming of our Lord Jesus Christ (1 Thess. 5:23–24). Sanctify me through and through, in this place, in this issue.

Healing the Brokenness

Now for the best part: the healing. God wants to make you whole and holy. He promises to heal the brokenhearted. So now you invite Jesus to heal the wound, to love you in this place, to restore your soul, to heal this memory. You invite Him into your past.

Lord Jesus, I invite You into my wounds and my brokenness. [Again, don't be vague and general; be very specific.] *Jesus, I invite You into the day I was abused. Come into my shattered heart, my shame, come into that moment in my life. I ask You to cleanse me here, to heal my broken heart and make me whole.*

Linger in this place in prayer. Listen. Pay attention. Often Jesus will bring up something necessary to your healing. For example, suddenly you feel the anger toward your abuser—Jesus is showing you that you need to forgive.

Jesus, I forgive my brother for abusing me. I release him from my rage and I give him over to You.

Sometimes you'll feel the shame and self-rejection.

Lord Jesus, come into this shame. I renounce self-rejection. I renounce despising myself because of all that has happened. I forgive myself as well. Come and heal me.

Sometimes you will feel the young places in your heart crying out for love or for protection.

Lord Jesus, gather the young and frightened place in my heart into Your loving arms. Come and find me here, in these very places. Gather my heart into Your love and make me whole.

As you are inviting Jesus into your wounds, what is so very beautiful is the fact that quite often—not every time, but more than you'll expect—Jesus will show you what He is doing; you will see Him come. Call it seeing with your mind's eye or Christ using your imagination or seeing with the eyes of your heart or your spirit—however you want to describe it. Often you will see Christ come back into your past. He may take you by the hand and lead you out of that room. You might see Him step between you and the one who wounded you, or He might simply tell you, "You are forgiven, you are safe, I love you."

Healing doesn't necessarily have to be dramatic. Oftentimes it is very quiet. Jesus simply comes as we invite Him to, and though we may not "see" Him or "hear" Him, He comes, and we sense a new peace or quietness in our souls. Our hearts feel better somehow. The important thing is for us to give Him permission to enter these wounded places, invite His healing love, and wait in prayer for Him to come. Do this with each memory of wounding, with each event (ask the Holy Spirit to guide you).

Often I will pray Isaiah 61 as I do this:

Lord Jesus, You have come to heal the brokenhearted, to proclaim freedom for the captives and release from darkness for the prisoners, to proclaim the year of the Lord's favor and the day of vengeance of our God. Come and heal my brokenness right here, Lord; free me from this captivity, release me from all darkness, bring Your favor here in my soul and bring Your vengeance here against my enemies.

Lord, You came to comfort all who mourn, and provide for those who grieve in Zion—to bestow on them a crown of beauty instead of ashes, the oil of gladness instead of mourning, and a garment of praise instead of a spirit of despair. I ask You to do this in me—comfort me where I am hurting; bestow on me a crown of beauty instead of ashes, the oil of gladness instead of mourning, and a garment of praise instead of a spirit of despair. Come in this memory, in this wound. I receive You here.

Many times, Jesus simply says, "Let Me love you." We need to open our hearts up to His love. As we do, it allows Him to come to this very place. Linger there and listen; ask for the healing grace of Jesus Christ over and over again. He comes, dear friends, He comes (Wild at Heart, 2013; Removing Chains, 2020; Wild at Heart, 2018).

SIGNS WHEN YOUR CHILD IS DEPRESSED

You may be wondering what depression looks like in a child or teen. The short answer: it looks pretty much like depression in an adult. This includes:

- ✓ Acting sad (moping around the house, slouched posture, unhappy facial expression)
- ✓ Crying frequently and easily provoked to tears
- ✓ Changes in sleep (this could be increased sleep, decreased sleep, problems getting to sleep, etc.)
- ✓ Changes in appetite (dramatic increases or reductions in appetite, often with changes in body weight).
- ✓ Lack of energy (they play less, move less, are harder to get moving into the car, to the dinner table, out of bed in the morning, etc.)
- ✓ Change in attention/concentration. Your child has gone from having adequate focus to having a difficult time concentrating on homework, or other subjects.
- ✓ Anhedonia. This is a Latin word. It means someone fails to feel pleasure in activities that had been (and normally are) pleasurable. (Pro Insight: We therapists are fond of Latin words, they help us feel we know something others don't). The idea with anhedonia is

that activities that used to be attention grabbing and pleasurable for the child are no longer of interest.
✓ Feeling helpless or hopeless.

You will find those same symptom features in adult depression. The one thing that often stands out differently with children, and often with adolescents, is that when depressed they have a tendency to act out, have tantrums and angry outbursts, in addition to the above symptoms.

Anyone looking over that list of symptoms is going to think, "Every child does these things from time to time. How do you know when these symptoms mean a kiddo is depressed?" Great question. Come to the front of the class.

Therapists generally refer to specific diagnostic criteria to make that determination. I'm not going to go into the intricacies of different symptoms, and duration of symptoms associated with different depressive disorders.

If your child has three of the symptoms listed above, and they have lasted two weeks or more, consult your pediatrician (Poland, 2020; Websites, 2021; Young, 2021; Talley, 2021).

HELP RESOURCES FOR TEENS AND YOUNG ADULTS

The National Suicide Prevention Lifeline at 800-273-TALK (8255)

Youth Talkline at 1-800-246-PRIDE (800-246-7743)

Trans Lifeline at 877-565-8860

The GLBT National Help Center at 1-888-THE-GLNH (888-843-4564)

The Crisis Call Center at 1-800-273-8255

TeenLine - www.teenlineonline.org 1800-852-8336 Text "TEEN" to 839863

The Samaritans Crisis Hotline at 1-212-673-3000

The National Sexual Assault Hotline at 1-800-656-4673

The National Domestic Violence Hotline at 1-800-799-7223

The National Crime Victim Helpline at 1-800-394-2255.

The important thing, though, is to make sure that whatever you're feeling or whatever your situation, keep in mind that someone out there can help, and someone out there will listen with kindness.

Struggling with Anxiety: Create your own profile at Anxiety Social Net (anxietysocialnet.com) to connect with people dealing with everything from social anxiety to agoraphobia. Prefer to meet in person? Find a state-by-state list of support groups at the Anxiety and Depression Association of America's website (adaa.org).

Struggling with Depression or Bipolar Disorder: Locate an in-person or online group at the Depression and Bipolar Support Alliance site (dbsalliance.org).

Struggling with Postpartum Depression: The Postpartum Progress site (postpartumprogress.com) lists support groups in nearly every state as well as in Canada and maintains an online forum.

Struggling with Schizophrenia: The Schizophrenia and Related Disorders Alliance of America facilitates groups nationwide; find one on its site (sardaa.org). You can also dial into its phone groups (855-640-8271) at 7 P.M. ET Sunday, Thursday and Friday with the pass code 88286491#.

Plagued by Obsessive-Compulsive Thoughts and Behaviors: More than 200 groups are listed with the International OCD Foundation (iocdf.org), which aids those affected by the disorder and their families.

The Adult Child of an Alcoholic: The Adult Children of Alcoholics World Service Organization maintains numerous support groups and hosts call-in and online sessions (meetings.adultchildren.org).

Grieving Someone Who Died by Suicide: Join one of the many groups for survivors listed on the American Foundation for Suicide Prevention website (afsp.org).

A Survivor of Rape, Sexual Assault or Incest: After Silence (aftersilence.org) is a message board and chat room for victims of sexual violence. Additionally, Adult Survivors of Child Abuse (ascasupport.org) organizes support groups around the U.S. and abroad, and offers resources for those who want to start their own.

Battling Anorexia, Bulimia, Binge Eating or Food Addiction: Eating Disorder Hope catalogs online support groups (eatingdisorderhope.com/recovery/support-groups/online); it also offers help and advice for those close to someone struggling to overcome an eating disorder.

Battling Sex Addiction: Sex Addicts Anonymous (saa-recovery.org), similar to Alcoholics Anonymous, offers a widespread network of in-person, online, and phone meetings.

Self-Harming: Daily Strength hosts a web forum where people dealing with self-injury can find encouragement, understanding, and a new way to cope (dailystrength.org/group/self-injury).

A Veteran Who Is Injured Or Has PTSD: The VA Combat Call Center—877-WAR-VETS (877-927-8387)—is staffed

24/7 by fellow combat veterans or spouses of disabled veterans who can offer immediate help; the Vet Center program site (vetcenter.va.gov) can direct visitors to both group and private counseling sessions in their area.

People often don't get the mental health services they need because they don't know where to start. Talk to your primary care doctor or another health professional about mental health problems. Ask them to connect you with the right mental health services. If you do not have a health professional who is able to assist you, use these resources to find help for yourself, your friends, your family, or your students.

Emergency Medical Services—911: If the situation is potentially life-threatening, get immediate emergency assistance by calling 911, available twenty-four hours a day.

National Suicide Prevention Lifeline, 1-800-273-TALK (8255) or Live Online Chat. If you or someone you know is suicidal or in emotional distress, contact the National Suicide Prevention Lifeline. Trained crisis workers are available to talk twenty-four hours a day, seven days a week. Your confidential and toll-free call goes to the nearest crisis center in the Lifeline national network. These centers provide crisis counseling and mental health referrals.

SAMHSA: Substance Abuse & Mental Health Services Administration Treatment Referral Helpline, 1-877-SAMHSA 7 (1-877-726-4727)

Get general information on mental health and locate treatment services in your area. Speak to a live person, Monday through Friday from 8 a.m. to 8 p.m. EST.

Mental Health America, formerly the National Mental Health Association, is a non-profit dedicated to improving the lives of people living with mental illness. The organization has offices and branches around the country, and a comprehensive "finding help" tool that includes self-assessment tools, links to finding someone in your community to talk to, and even tips on how to make the most of your relationship with a therapist or social worker, as well as a crisis number you can call in case of emergency (1-800-273-TALK).

Additionally, Mental Health America offers resources beyond just therapy and medication—they'll help with other aspects of your life as well that may be impacted by mental health issues, for as long as it exists, serves as a catch-all location for mental health programs, resources, and even studies and evidence-based articles that can help you find someone to talk to. There are detailed pieces on what to look for in yourself or someone you know that may be an indicator that person is dealing with an undiagnosed issue, and even resources for people who know a loved one who's in treatment or could use help, and how to handle their own feelings about that.

Whether you need immediate help, you're a veteran struggling with PTSD or another mental health challenge, or you're just looking for information on how to manage the complex web of health insurance and mental health offerings, there are resources to help you. They even have an easily bookmarkable page with hotlines and live chat worth keeping on-hand if you or someone else is ever in a dark spot.

The Trevor Project provides crisis intervention and suicide prevention for LGBTQ youth, in the form of its hotline (1-866-488-7386) and text line (Text "Trevor" to 1-202-304-1200), its social network (called TrevorSpace,) its support center articles, and online chat. You can get a quick rundown of the options here, and their operating hours (the hotline is 24/7, for the record.)

In addition to the hotline though, the support center offers a wealth of resources and deep reading on a variety of topics, including coming out to family or struggling with their own identity, as well as other mental health issues like depression or bipolar disorder, or those contemplating self-harm. They're also happy to accept volunteers or donations, and have a great series of videos designed to help people become "lifeguards," or learn how to help at-risk LGBTQ teenagers

IAMAlive is an online crisis network, and all of its volunteers are professionally supervised and trained in crisis prevention. Unlike many services (some of which are helpful and we'll name later) where the listeners are volunteers or people just willing to lend an open ear, IAMAlive volunteers are trained to help you in almost any situation and can help you find additional in-person resources to help as well. The **Crisis Text Line**, which we've highlighted before, is a 24/7 service that's text only. Right now though, their website is absolutely packed with support numbers and additional information. Plus, texting lets you reach out when you're away from home or a computer, feeling unsafe about accepting or placing a phone call, or discreetly if you need to. Simply text 741-741 with the message "START" to get started. You'll have to provide a couple of details, but after that you're connected with someone who can help.

BlahTherapy offers a combination of free and premium services that will give you people to chat with if you need someone to talk to. On the free side, you can speak anonymously to a listener at any time without signing up or registering for the site. It's a bit like venting to a stranger who's willing to listen—don't expect comprehensive help or anything, but sometimes it's nice to just be heard by someone who has an open ear.

On the premium side though, BlahTherapy can connect you with actual therapists and social workers who can talk to you via live chat, after being matched with someone who can help with the things you're feeling or the issues you're facing. It's a chat relationship, of course, but they're absolutely willing to help. You can try the premium service out for a week before you have to sign up for a subscription.

Youth and Adolescents Resources

Call 1.800.784.2433, the **National Hopeline Network.** You'll be connected automatically to a certified Crisis Center near your location. Crisis Center calls are answered by trained counselors twenty-four hours a day, seven days a week. In the event that the nearest Crisis Center is at maximum volume, the call is seamlessly rerouted to the next closest center. Callers should never encounter a busy signal or voice mail. For easy recall, remember this: 1.800.SUICIDE. hopeline.com

Call 1.800.273.8255, the **National Suicide Prevention Lifeline**, which also provides access to trained telephone counselors, twenty-four hours a day, seven days a week. For easy recall, think 1.800.273.TALK. For the same help in Spanish; call 1.888.628.9454. Individuals who are deaf or hard of hearing can contact the lifeline via TTY, at: 1.800.799.4889. suicidepreventionlifeline.org

Visit the **American Association of Suicidology** (AAS) online. AAC is dedicated to the understanding and prevention of suicide. For those seeking info and perspective on this difficult subject, including the warning signs and guidance on what to do, the association offers many publications that can help. www.suicidology.org

Find a residential placement for an individual. **The Association of Children's Residential Centers** concerns itself with therapeutic living environments for children and adolescents with behavioral health disorders. You can take a look at ACRC's member list to see what types of residential centers are available to help children who need this sort of residence. Find these detailed descriptions online at: togetherthevoice.org/our-members

A Quick-Read Fact Sheet. If you're looking for an intro to emotional problems and the mental health field, this is a good place to start. This fact sheet will hook you up with organizations that can help, online and print resources for more information, and an overview look at disabilities that cause mental health concerns. www.parentcenterhub.org/repository/emotionaldisturbance

There are numerous sources of incredible information, support, and guidance on mental illness—

National Federation of Families for Children's Mental Health (NFFCMH). The link below takes you to a wealth of resources for parents on specific mental health diagnoses as well as and other topics related to children's health and family involvement in systems that impact children. www.ffcmh.org/resources

MentalHealth.gov. MentalHealth.gov provides one-stop access to U.S. government mental health and mental health problems information. www.mentalhealth.gov

NAMI, the National Alliance for the Mentally Ill. NAMI calls itself the "Nation's Voice on Mental Illness" and is an invaluable source of information on the subject. In addition to the mountain of info you'll find on NAMI's site, you can also connect with state and local NAMI chapters. www.nami.org

Mental Health America. NMHA addresses all aspects of mental health and mental illness. Delve into their online resources about mental issues and identify NMHA affiliates in your area. www.nmha.org

American Academy of Child and Adolescent Psychiatry (AACAP). At the link below, you can find information on child and adolescent psychiatry, fact sheets for parents and caregivers, current research, practice guidelines, and managed care information, among other things. www.aacap.org

Gay, Lesbian and Straight Education Network: GLSEN is the leading national education organization focused on ensuring safe schools for all students. This website provides resources on finding GSA Chapters, and tools on how to establish or reestablish a GSA. http://www.glsen.org/

StopBullying.Gov: This website offers resources specifically for teens to prevent bullying in their schools and communities and provides resources for those being bullied. http://www.stopbullying.gov/

Teens Against Bullying: Created by and for teens, this website is a place for middle and high school students to find ways to address bullying, take action, be heard, and own an important social cause. http://www.pacerteensagainstbullying.org

(Mental Health Resources for People in Crisis, 2019; Mental Health Resources for Teenagers, 2021; What Teens Need During a Pandemic, 2020; Mental Health Resources that are Absolutely Free, 2021).

APPS AND TECH SERVICES

Beacon 2.0: Beacon is a portal to online applications (websites, mobile applications and internet support groups) for mental disorders reviewed and rated by health experts. https://beacon.anu.edu.au/

Health Talk: This website reflects the lived experience of mental health conditions, including research-based modules with hours of recording and analysis. www.healthtalk.org/peoples-experiences/mental-health

Mindfulness for Teens: This website has resources to help teens use mindfulness to handle stress and includes apps to practice meditation and guided meditation recordings. http://mindfulnessforteens.com/

Mood 247: A text messaging system that provides an easy way to record how you're feeling and tracks your daily moods to share with friends, family, or a health professional. https://www.mood247.com/

Strength of Us: An online community designed to inspire young adults impacted by mental health issues to think positive, stay strong, and achieve goals through peer support and resource sharing. http://strengthofus.org/

RESOURCES: Teens

Center for Young Women's Health and Young Men's Health: These websites provide a series of guides on emotional health, including on test anxiety, depression, bullying, and eating disorders. www.youngwomenshealth.org and www.young-menshealthsite.org

Go Ask Alice!: Geared toward young adults, this question and answer website contains a large database of questions about a variety of concerns surrounding emotional health. www.goaskalice.columbia.edu

Girls Health.Gov: The "Your Feelings" section of this website offers guidance to teenage girls on recognizing a mental health problem, getting help, and talking to parents. http://girlshealth.gov/feelings/index.html

Jed Foundation: Promoting emotional health and preventing suicide among college students, this website provides an online resource center, ULifeline, a public dialogue forum, Half of Us, and Transition Year, resources and tools to help students transition to college. http://www.jedfoundation.org/students

Kelty Mental Health Resource Center: Reference sheets are provided that list top websites, books, videos, toolkits and support for mental health disorders. http://keltymentalhealth.ca/youth-and-young-adults

Reach Out: This website provides information on specific mental health disorders, as well as resources to help teens make safe plans when feeling suicidal, and helpful tips on how to relax. http://au.reachout.com/

Teens Health: Providing a safe place for teens who need honest and accurate information, this website provides resources on mental health issues. http://teenshealth.org/teen/your_mind/

Teen Mental Health: Geared towards teenagers, this website provides learning tools on a variety of mental illnesses, videos, and resources for friends. http://teenmentalhealth.org/

International Crisis Hotlines - www.removingchains.org

United Kingdom - Survivors of Bereavement by Suicide Call: 0844 477 9400 everyday 9:00am - 9:00pm

C.A.L.L. Mental Health Helpline Wales - Call: 0800 132 737 or ext, "help" to 81066

Counselling Directory UK Samaritans Call: 08457 90 90 90

Suicide Hotlines Papyrus Hopeline UK Call: 0800 068 41 41 SMS: 07786 209697

National Bullying Helpline Call: 0845 22 55 787

Refuge National Domestic Violence Helpline Call: 0808 2000 24

Eating Disorder Hotlines - Beat Helplines Call: 0808 801 0677 - **Studentline** Call: 0808 801 0811

Anxiety Support UK - Call: 0844 477 5774

Emergency Dial: 999

FOODS THAT IMPROVE DEPRESSION

Walnuts are a very good source of omega-3 fatty acids. These have been shown to be able to support the functioning of the brain and can also help to reduce depression. The fact that many modern diets don't include these compounds could be contributing to increasing cases of depression.

Tomatoes are a good source of folic acid and alpha-lipoic acid, and both of these have been shown to be effective at fighting depression. Indeed, some studies have shown there is a correlation between folate deficiency and depression. Tomatoes can help prevent such deficiencies and help to keep depression at bay as a result.

Leafy greens are among the most nutrient-rich foods available to us. They are generally packed full of vitamins and minerals in quantities. What's more, leafy greens may also be able to help prevent depression. Most types have anti-inflammatories that can help prevent inflammation of the brain, which is at fault for depression in many cases. They also help to keep the immune system strong, and this too will help our overall physical and mental well-being.

Blueberries. The vitamins in blueberries can help to boost our immune system, and keeping free from disease can help prevent depression from setting in. They are also a very good source of antioxidants, and these too can help to prevent depression from developing.

Blueberries are truly incredible little berries. Not only do they contain iron, magnesium, and potassium, they also reduce pain, are anti-inflammatory agents and increase the production of dopamine, which is the brain's feel-good chemical. You can expect to be in a feel-good mood about an hour after drinking your smoothie. Dopamine is a hormone associated with happiness, and serotonin regulates our moods. This hormone reduces pain perception and increases the emotional connection that we are in a positive mood.

Avocados are packed full of nutrition and are often found in healthy-living diets, despite their high fat and calorie content. They can also help to treat and prevent depression. Avocados are a great source of omega-3 fatty acids and this means they are good for the brain. They are also a good source of oleic acid, which also helps to promote a healthy brain.

Blueberry Avocado Smoothie

This smoothie has a bold blueberry flavor that is very nourishing. The healthy fats from the avocado support brain health and nourish your body to keep you feeling full!

To make this blueberry avocado smoothie, you'll need the following ingredients:
Blueberries (fresh or frozen) 1cup
Avocado half (get frozen if possible)
Banana (I recommend frozen) 1
Kale (handful)
Plant-based milk - Almond or Cashew Milk
Hemp seeds - (2tsp)
Then, add everything to your blender. Blend it up, and enjoy (Avocadocentric, 2020)!

Green tea contains an amino acid called theanine that may affect secretion of serotonin and other neurotransmitters, including the calming neurotransmitter GABA and the activating neurotransmitters dopamine, epinephrine and norepinephrine. Its main effects are to increase levels of GABA and dopamine, which increases your sense of well-being

I can definitely confirm the effects of the blueberry avocado smoothie and the positive effects of drinking green tea. These are great for kids, too. Mood-boosting and brain-empowering foods are needed for our mental health as well as our physical health. Greens like spinach and kale are very important as well, and if you're someone like me, who isn't too big on eating greens all the time, they are great in smoothies because all the fruit overpowers the taste and you get all the health benefits.

I've found that foods rich in omega fatty acids really do improve my mood and help me cope with tough days. Foods like nuts and seeds (such as flaxseed, chia seeds, and walnuts) really boost your omega 3 and 6 intake, which is so important to mental health.

Before bed, I love to get a cup of chamomile tea with honey. It calms my nerves and helps me fall asleep faster.

Healthy Meal I Recommend for Boosting Mood!

Ratatouille.
<Lol> Don't laugh, and yes I got this from the Disney movie, but it's a great recipe.

Ingredients:
3 Zucchini
2 Red or Orange Bell Peppers
Ragu Pasta Sauce: Chunky Garden
Himalayan pink salt
Basil and rosemary seasoning.

Instructions: Clean veggies, slice zucchini thin, like you're chopping carrots, for example. Slice the bell peppers thin. Lay all the zucchini in a circle-like layer. Place sliced bell peppers on top. Season with a few dashes of the Himalayan pink salt and a few dashes of the basil and rosemary seasoning. Add Ragu pasta sauce and spread it on thick and even.

Preheat the oven to 400°. Place the pan in the oven for 25-35mins. After it's done, let it cool for 10 minutes and enjoy.

This with a blueberry avocado smoothie is awesome (Lake, 2019).

CONCLUSION

We live in a very selfish world where so many people have lost love, care and concern for others, and they feel good knocking the next person down.

Well, I'm here to tell you that you matter, You have a purpose. You are unique, and you are here on this earth for a reason. It doesn't matter who is against you, who doesn't like you, who doesn't like the way you look. Remind yourself: you matter, you have a purpose and these people who have all these negative things to say about you are irrelevant to your future and irrelevant to your life.

Their opinion doesn't define who you are. Even when you have negative thoughts about yourself, remind yourself you matter: you matter to your family, you matter to the people who care about you, and you matter because you have a right to be happy in your own skin. We cannot accept every negative voice that speaks over us. We have to reject the negativity, mental negativity we bring on ourselves and outside negativity from other people.

Don't be defined by what someone else thinks about you. Be defined by who you are and who you are working to be. I want you to reflect on a few things that have troubled you in your past and things that are troubling you now. Take out your journal and write down these feelings and issues that give you moments of sadness, regret, fear, shame or pain. This method helps to release pain from your past. In a sense, you are getting the emotions out of your head and heart and releasing them to the paper. This helps reduce anxiety by allowing your mind to be relieved of all the buildup over the years. Keeping a book where you can write down your experiences helps give you a voice and release pain.

To the beautiful people reading these words, I want to say to you that I'm grateful for you. I am proud of you. I believe in you. You have abilities, talents and gifts. I believe you have a future. There is hope for you. You can make it and you can definitely get through anything that is causing you pain and struggle. You are loved. You are important. You are special. You are unique. You are creative.

Your family needs you. Your friends need you. You are smart. You are inventive. I know you can accomplish great things. You are more than the negative names people have called you. Jesus loves you and accepts you just the way you are. There is nothing you have done that can stop God from loving you. You can go to God with confidence no matter how wrong you have been. No matter how hurt you are.

You are accepted and welcomed by the Lord. All you have to do is go to God and ask for help and Jesus will help you! You are the apple of God's eye. He knows the number of hairs on your head. He knew you before you were born. He made you on purpose for a purpose. You are not an accident, but a precious person planned by God. You are more than you know. When you go to God to understand who you truly are, you begin to discover every amazing part of God's plan for you. You were beautifully and wonderfully made. You are a treasure and life is polishing you, take God's hand to become all you were designed to be.

VICTORY

Jeremiah 29:11 – For I know the plans I have for you," declares the Lord, "plans to prosper you and not to harm you, plans to give you hope and a future."

REFERENCES

Avocadocentric, & Avocadocentric, A. (2020, August 21). Blueberry Avocado Smoothie (Vegan & Gluten free). Retrieved November 12, 2020, from https://avocado-centric.com/blueberry-avocado-smoothie/

Fowler, J. A. (Writer). (2019, December 16). Powerful or Powerless [Video file]. Retrieved February 14, 2020, from @juliaafowler

Lake, James. M.D. (2019, August 17). "Foods That Have Antidepressant Effects." *Psychology Today,* Retrieved November 12, 2020, from https://www.psychologytoday.com/us/blog/integrative-mental-health-care/201908/foods-have-antidepressant-effects

Mental Health Resources for People in Crisis. (2019, May 23). *Psycom,* Retrieved January 08, 2021, from https://www.psycom.net/get-help-mental-health

Mental Health Resources for Teenagers. (n.d.). Retrieved January 08, 2021, from https://online.maryville.edu/online-bachelors-degrees/psychology/mental-health-resources-teenagers/

Prayer for Freedom from Habitual Sins: Wild at Heart. (2013, April 24). Retrieved November 12, 2020, from https://wildatheart.org/prayer/prayer-freedom-habitual-sins

Removing Chains is Listeners Reviving Hearts with Hope. (n.d.). *Removing Chains,* Retrieved November 12, 2020, from https://www.removingchains.org/

Shareable Resources on Suicide Prevention. (n.d.). Retrieved November 12, 2020, from https://www.nimh.nih.gov/health/education-awareness/shareable-resources-on-suicide-prevention.shtml

Staff of Parenting Alpha. . (2020, September 05). "How to Tell Your Child is Depressed and Needs Help! *Parenting Alpha,* Retrieved November 12, 2020, from https://parentingalpha.com/how-to-tell-your-child-is-depressed-and-needs-help/

Talley, Forrest. (2019, August 14). "Important Signs of Child/Teen Depression - And How To Turn Things Around." *Forest Talley,* Retrieved January 08, 2021, from https://forresttalley.com/blog-anxiety-depression-trauma-ptsd-positivepsychology/yu2Ojawqhzyugain7wo8lbtgOky2xz?format=amp

Top HelpLine Resources. (n.d.). Retrieved January 08, 2021, from https://www.nami.org/Support-Education/NAMI-HelpLine/Top-HelpLine-Resources

University, N. (n.d.). Scott Poland: College of Psychology. Retrieved December 29, 2020, from https://psychology.nova.edu/faculty/profile/poland.html

Websites Especially for Teens. (n.d.). Retrieved January 08, 2021, from https://interface.williamjames.edu/guide/websites-especially-teens

Unger, Michael, Ph.D. (2020, Mar. 25) "What Teens Need During a Pandemic" *Psychology Today*. (n.d.). Retrieved November 12, 2020, from https://www.psychology-today.com/us/blog/nurturing-resilience/202003/what-teens-need-during-pandemic

Wild at Heart UK - Letter from the Team: Wild at Heart. (2018, April 03). Retrieved November 12, 2020, from https://www.ransomedheart.com/wild-heart-uk-letter-team

Young, Karen, Tony February 28th, Gin ksai February 20th, Karen Young February 27th, Christine February 16th, Karen Young February 17th,…*, N. (2020, August 13). Depression in Teens: The Warning Signs and How to Help Them Through. Retrieved November 12, 2020, from https://www.heysigmund.com/depression-teens-warning-signs-help/comment-page-1/13 Mental Health Resources that Are Absolutely Free. (n.d.). Retrieved January 08, 2021, from http://www.oprah.com/omagazine/free-online-resources-for-mental-illness

Young, Karen (n.d.). Depression Archives. https://www.heysigmund.com/the-question-that-could-save-a-life-depressed/

CPSIA information can be obtained
at www.ICGtesting.com
Printed in the USA
JSHW031537160521
14664JS00004B/84